State Management with React Query

Improve developer and user experience by mastering server state in React

Daniel Afonso

‹packt›

BIRMINGHAM—MUMBAI

State Management with React Query

Copyright © 2023 Packt Publishing

All rights reserved. No part of this book may be reproduced, stored in a retrieval system, or transmitted in any form or by any means, without the prior written permission of the publisher, except in the case of brief quotations embedded in critical articles or reviews.

Every effort has been made in the preparation of this book to ensure the accuracy of the information presented. However, the information contained in this book is sold without warranty, either express or implied. Neither the author, nor Packt Publishing or its dealers and distributors, will be held liable for any damages caused or alleged to have been caused directly or indirectly by this book.

Packt Publishing has endeavored to provide trademark information about all of the companies and products mentioned in this book by the appropriate use of capitals. However, Packt Publishing cannot guarantee the accuracy of this information.

Group Product Manager: Pavan Ramchandani
Publishing Product Manager: Jane D'Souza
Senior Editor: Mark D'Souza
Technical Editor: Simran Udasi
Copy Editor: Safis Editing
Project Coordinator: Manthan Patel
Proofreader: Safis Editing
Indexer: Sejal Dsilva
Production Designer: Joshua Misquitta
Marketing Coordinators: Namita Velgekar, Nivedita Pandey, and Anamika Singh

First published: May 2023
Production reference: 2250423

Published by Packt Publishing Ltd.
Livery Place
35 Livery Street
Birmingham
B3 2PB, UK.

ISBN 978-1-80323-134-1

www.packtpub.com

To my parents, for always supporting me and teaching me not to give up and to work for my dreams. To my brother, you are amazing and have a bright future ahead of you. To my friends, for putting up with me throughout all these years. To my soon-to-be wife, Mariana, for keeping me grounded, for all your love, and, most importantly, for never giving up on me.

– Daniel Afonso

Foreword

I got to know *Daniel Afonso* when I joined Talkdesk at the end of 2020 as an Agile coach, supporting two teams. I was fortunate enough to work with Daniel, who was then a software developer in one of these teams.

The first thing I noticed about him was his enthusiasm, positive energy, and optimism. You couldn't help but feel enthusiastic with him around (and the fact that we were all working remotely didn't change anything)! I've worked in IT for 24 years, 16 of those in Agile and Lean – I can tell you that if everyone I've met in my professional life had this kind of drive and enthusiasm, I would be out of a job by now.

The second thing that I've noticed? Daniel was, is, and (from what I can see) will continue to be a lifelong learner. The so-called "comfort zone" is uncomfortable for him – if he's not learning/doing something new, he gets bored. I'm like that too. So, despite our age gap (I recall when we were chatting one day and discovered that I am a year younger than Daniel's mother), we "clicked" very quickly. I don't have many friends, nor do I use the word "friend" lightly – but I am very grateful to count Daniel as one of my friends.

From then on, Daniel did what the rising stars do. And he's still rising.

He currently works as a developer advocate, the role he's always wanted. It takes a very particular mix of skills to be a great developer advocate – you need to be great technically and be an excellent communicator. Not an easy combination to find in the wild, but that's exactly what Daniel is.

Daniel starts this book by focusing on states and why most apps nowadays are based on states. He proceeds to describe the distinction between client and server states.

After this, he dives into the challenges of changing server states and introduces a new way to deal with them: React Query.

From then, Daniel extensively shows how to use React Query to its full potential, including for data-fetching, mutations, and testing.

Do yourself a favor and enjoy Daniel Afonso's masterclass – I am sure you will not regret the time invested.

Ricardo Mestre

Director of Agile Operations, Talkdesk

Contributors

About the author

Daniel Afonso is a developer advocate with a full-stack background, having worked with different languages and frameworks on various projects, from IoT to fraud detection. He is passionate about learning and teaching and has spoken at multiple conferences related to React, JavaScript, and testing. In his free time, when he's not learning new technologies or writing about them, he's probably reading comics or watching superhero movies and shows.

Thank you to everyone that supported me throughout this journey. Thank you to André Simões and Ricardo Mestre for accepting the invite and joining this adventure with me. Thank you to Mariana for all the understanding and support throughout all the days I had to spend writing.

About the reviewers

André Simões is a passionate frontend engineer who likes to work with cutting-edge technologies and provide smart solutions for challenging problems. He has ~15 years of experience in architecting and developing thoroughly tested web apps and building teams from the ground up. Currently working with React, he has an interest in topics such as state management, micro frontends, and everything that may benefit the end user and/or dev experience.

Paul Blyth is a software engineer with 15 years of professional experience as a core contributor to, and leading teams responsible for, multimillion-dollar web applications for companies such as British Airways, Couchbase, and Spotify. Paul is an advocate for React Query and the huge benefits it brings, having introduced it into large production apps to enrich the UX and streamline code complexity.

Table of Contents

Preface i

Part 1: Understanding State and Getting to Know React Query

1

What Is State and How Do We Manage It? 3

Technical requirements	4	Sharing state with React Context	10
What is state in React?	4	What do different state management libraries have in common?	12
Managing state in React	5		
Managing state with useState	6	Summary	13
Managing state with useReducer	8		

2

Server State versus Client State 15

Technical requirements	16	Caching	22
What is global state?	16	Optimistic updates	22
What is client state?	19	Deduping requests	23
What is server state?	20	Performance optimization	23
Understanding common challenges with server state	22	Summary	24

3

React Query – Introducing, Installing, and Configuring It — 25

Technical requirements	26	Script tag	29
What is React Query?	26	Configuring React Query	29
Query	26	QueryClient	30
Mutation	27	QueryClientProvider	34
How does React Query solve my server state challenges?	27	Adding React Query Devtools	34
Installing React Query	28	Floating Mode	35
npm	28	Embedded Mode	37
Yarn	29	Enabling Devtools in your production build	38
pnpm	29	Summary	40

Part 2: Managing Server State with React Query

4

Fetching Data with React Query — 43

Technical requirements	43	Refetching data with useQuery	61
What is useQuery and how does it work?	44	Automatic refetching	61
		Manual refetching	63
What is a query key?	44	Fetching dependent queries with useQuery	64
What is a query function?	46		
What does useQuery return?	51	Putting it all into practice	65
Commonly used options explained	57	Summary	71

5

More Data-Fetching Challenges — 73

Technical requirements	74	Dynamic parallel queries	75
Building parallel queries	74	Leveraging QueryClient	76
Manual parallel queries	74	Query invalidation	78

Prefetching	80	Creating infinite queries	90
Query cancelation	82	Debugging your queries with Devtools	94
Creating paginated queries	86	Summary	98

6
Performing Data Mutations with React Query   99

Technical requirements	100	How to perform an additional side effect	119
What is useMutation and how does it work?	100	How to retrigger a query refetch after mutation	121
What is the mutation function?	100	How to perform an update to our query data after a mutation	122
What does useMutation return?	103		
Commonly used mutation options explained	115	Performing optimistic updates	123
Performing side-effect patterns after mutations	119	Summary	127

7
Server-Side Rendering with Next.js or Remix   129

Technical requirements	130	Applying the initialData pattern in Remix	132
Why should I use React Query with server-side rendering frameworks?	130	Using the hydrate pattern	134
Using the initialData pattern	131	Applying the hydrate pattern in Next.js	135
Applying the initialData pattern in Next.js	131	Applying the hydrate pattern in Remix	137
		Summary	141

8
Testing React Query Hooks and Components   143

Technical requirements	144	Organizing code	147
Configuring Mock Service Worker	144	Creating an API file	147
		Leveraging query key factories	148

Creating a hooks folder	149	Testing mutations	171
Testing components that use React Query	**151**	**Testing custom hooks that use React Query**	**176**
Setting up testing utils	151	**Summary**	**184**
Testing queries	153		

9

What Changes in React Query v5? 185

Technical requirements	186	Next.js hydrate pattern renaming	189
What are the support changes?	186	Remix hydrate pattern changes	190
Using only the object format	186	Removing keepPreviousData and using placeholderData	191
Removing the logger	187		
Renaming loading to pending	188	Introducing a new way to perform optimistic updates	192
Renaming cacheTime to gcTime	189		
Renaming Hydrate to HydrationBoundary	189	Introducing maxPages to infinite queries	197
		Summary	**198**

Index 201

Other Books You May Enjoy 208

Preface

State management is one of the hottest topics in the React ecosystem. There are many libraries and tools for handling state in React, and with each comes different recipes and opinions. One thing is clear – state management solutions for handling client state are not so good at dealing with server state. React Query was created as a solution to help manage your server state!

In *State Management with React Query*, you will get a guide that will take you from zero to hero with React Query by the end of the book.

You'll begin by learning the historical background of state in the React world and what led to the need to change from global state to client and server state. With this knowledge under your belt, you will understand the need for React Query. As you advance through the chapters, you'll learn how React Query helps you to deal with common server state challenges, such as fetching data, caching data, updating data, and synchronizing your data with the server.

But this is not all – once you have mastered React Query, you will learn how to apply this knowledge to server-side rendering.

Finally, you will learn some patterns for testing your code by leveraging the Testing Library and Mock Service Worker.

By the end of this book, you'll have a new perspective on state and be able to leverage React Query to solve all the challenges of server state in your applications.

Who this book is for

This book is for JavaScript and React developers who want to improve their state management skills and start dealing with the challenges of server state, while improving their developer and user experience.

Basic knowledge of web development, JavaScript, and React will help with understanding some of the key concepts covered in this book.

What this book covers

Chapter 1, *What Is State and How Do We Manage It?*, covers a basic definition of what state is and gives a historical overview of how we manage it.

Chapter 2, *Server State versus Client State*, splits the state concept and helps us understand why it is so important to manage the server state independently of the client state.

Chapter 3, *React Query – Introducing, Installing, and Configuring It*, introduces React Query and provides the means to add it to your applications.

Chapter 4, *Fetching Data with React Query*, covers what you need to leverage the `useQuery` custom hook to fetch your server state.

Chapter 5, *More Data-Fetching Challenges*, expands on the concepts introduced in the previous chapter and covers how you can leverage `useQuery` to deal with other data fetching challenges.

Chapter 6, *Performing Data Mutations with React Query*, covers what you need to leverage the `useMutation` custom hook to perform changes on the server state.

Chapter 7, *Server-Side Rendering with Next.js or Remix*, covers leveraging React Query with server-side frameworks such as Next.js or Remix.

Chapter 8, *Testing React Query Hooks and Components*, provides you with practices and recipes you can apply to your application to test your components and custom hooks that leverage React Query.

Chapter 9, *What Changes in React Query v5?*, is a bonus chapter that covers the changes that the v5 version of TanStack Query introduces to React Query and the things you need to update your application.

To get the most out of this book

Basic knowledge of RESTful APIs and HTTP methods is recommended. Basic knowledge of GraphQL is required if you want to leverage the examples that use it.

You will need to know some of the basic concepts around HTML. You will also need to understand JavaScript and some of its concepts, namely promises.

Finally, given that we are using React Hooks, it is important that you are familiar with how they work and how you can use them in your React application.

Software/hardware covered in the book	Operating system requirements
Yarn	Windows, macOS, or Linux
pnpm	Windows, macOS, or Linux
npm	Windows, macOS, or Linux
JavaScript	Windows, macOS, or Linux
React 16.8	Windows, macOS, or Linux
Remix	Windows, macOS, or Linux
Next.js	Windows, macOS, or Linux
React Testing Library	Windows, macOS, or Linux

Mock Service Worker	Windows, macOS, or Linux
TanStack Query	Windows, macOS, or Linux

If you are using the digital version of this book, we advise you to type the code yourself or access the code from the book's GitHub repository (a link is available in the next section). Doing so will help you avoid any potential errors related to the copying and pasting of code.

This book gives you the practices and tools to fully understand and master the TanStack Query React adapter – React Query. By the end of the book, you will have the necessary understanding of how to leverage it fully and be set to decide whether you want to add it to your projects.

Download the example code files

You can download the example code files for this book from GitHub at https://github.com/PacktPublishing/State-management-with-React-Query. If there's an update to the code, it will be updated in the GitHub repository.

We also have other code bundles from our rich catalog of books and videos available at https://github.com/PacktPublishing/. Check them out!

Download the color images

We also provide a PDF file that has color images of the screenshots and diagrams used in this book. You can download it here: https://packt.link/Wt1n6.

Conventions used

There are a number of text conventions used throughout this book.

`Code in text`: Indicates code words in text, database table names, folder names, filenames, file extensions, pathnames, dummy URLs, user input, and Twitter handles. Here is an example: "Natively, React gives us two ways to hold state in our applications – `useState` and `useReducer`."

A block of code is set as follows:

```
const NotState = ({aList = [1, 2, 3, 4, 5, 6, 7, 8, 9, 10]}) =>
{
  const value = "a constant value";
  const filteredList = aList.filter((item) => item % 2 === 0);
```

```
  return filteredList.map((item) => <div key={item}>{item}</
div>);
};
```

When we wish to draw your attention to a particular part of a code block, the relevant lines or items are set in bold:

```
const App = () => {
  ...
  return (
    <div className="App">
      <div>Counter: {count}</div>
      <div>
        <button onClick={increment}>+1</button>
        <button onClick={decrement}>-1</button>
        <button onClick={reset}>Reset</button>
      </div>
    </div>
```

Any command-line input or output is written as follows:

```
npm i @tanstack/react-query
```

Bold: Indicates a new term, an important word, or words that you see on screen. For instance, words in menus or dialog boxes appear in **bold**. Here is an example: "As a user, I want my query to be re-fetched when I click the **Invalidate Query** button."

> **Tips or important notes**
> Appear like this.

Get in touch

Feedback from our readers is always welcome.

General feedback: If you have questions about any aspect of this book, email us at customercare@packtpub.com and mention the book title in the subject of your message.

Errata: Although we have taken every care to ensure the accuracy of our content, mistakes do happen. If you have found a mistake in this book, we would be grateful if you would report this to us. Please visit www.packtpub.com/support/errata and fill in the form.

Piracy: If you come across any illegal copies of our works in any form on the internet, we would be grateful if you would provide us with the location address or website name. Please contact us at `copyright@packt.com` with a link to the material.

If you are interested in becoming an author: If there is a topic that you have expertise in and you are interested in either writing or contributing to a book, please visit `authors.packtpub.com`.

Share your thoughts

Once you've read *State Management with React Query*, we'd love to hear your thoughts! Scan the QR code below to go straight to the Amazon review page for this book and share your feedback.

`https://packt.link/r/1-803-23134-3`

Your review is important to us and the tech community and will help us make sure we're delivering excellent quality content.

Download a free PDF copy of this book

Thanks for purchasing this book!

Do you like to read on the go but are unable to carry your print books everywhere?

Is your eBook purchase not compatible with the device of your choice?

Don't worry, now with every Packt book you get a DRM-free PDF version of that book at no cost.

Read anywhere, any place, on any device. Search, copy, and paste code from your favorite technical books directly into your application.

The perks don't stop there, you can get exclusive access to discounts, newsletters, and great free content in your inbox daily

Follow these simple steps to get the benefits:

1. Scan the QR code or visit the link below

```
https://packt.link/free-ebook/9781803231341
```

2. Submit your proof of purchase
3. That's it! We'll send your free PDF and other benefits to your email directly

Part 1: Understanding State and Getting to Know React Query

State is what makes your applications move. What many of us are not often aware of is that there are different types of state. These different types lead to different challenges when managing the given state. In this part, we will understand more about state and how we manage it. During this process, we will understand that the server and client states have very different challenges that need to be handled separately and with different tools. To deal with server state, we will learn more about the TanStack Query React adapter called React Query and see how to add it to our applications.

This part includes the following chapters:

- Chapter 1, What Is State and How Do We Manage It?
- Chapter 2, Server State versus Client State
- Chapter 3, React Query – Introducing, Installing, and Configuring It

1
What Is State and How Do We Manage It?

State is a mutable data source that can be used to store data in a **React** application and can change over time and be used to determine how your component renders.

This chapter will refresh your existing knowledge about state in the React ecosystem. We will review what it is and why it is needed, and understand how it helps you build React applications.

We'll also review how you can manage state natively in React by using the **useState** hook, the **useReducer** hook, and **React Context**.

Finally, we'll offer brief descriptions of the common state management solutions such as **Redux**, **Zustand**, and **MobX** and understand why they have been created and the main common concept they all share.

By the end of this chapter, you will have either learned or remembered everything about state necessary to proceed in this book. You will also notice a pattern in how state is managed between different state management solutions and meet or get reacquainted with a familiar term. Spoiler alert: it is global state.

In this chapter, we'll be covering the following topics:

- What is state in React?
- Managing state in React
- What do different state management libraries have in common?

Technical requirements

In this book, you are going to see some code snippets. If you want to try them out, you are going to need the following:

- An **integrated development environment** (**IDE**) such as Visual Studio Code.
- A web browser (Google Chrome, Firefox, or Edge).
- Node.js. All the code in this book was written with the current LTS version installed (16.16.0).
- A package manager (npm, Yarn, or pnpm).
- A React project. If you don't have one, you can create one with Create React App by running the following command in your terminal:

  ```
  npx create-react-app my-react-app
  ```

All the code examples for this chapter can be found on GitHub at https://github.com/PacktPublishing/State-management-with-React-Query/tree/feat/chapter_1.

What is state in React?

State is the heart of your React application.

I challenge you to try to build a React application without any type of state. You'd probably be able to do something, but you would soon conclude that props cannot do everything for you and get stuck.

As mentioned in the introduction, state is a mutable data source used to store your data.

State is mutable, which means that it can be changed over time. When a state variable changes, your React component will re-render to reflect any changes that the state causes to your UI.

Okay, now, you might be wondering, *"What will I store in my state?"* Well, the rule of thumb that I follow is that if your data fits into any of the following points, then it's not state:

- Props
- Data that will always be the same
- Data that can be derived from other state variables or props

Anything that doesn't fit this list can be stored in state. This means things such as data you just fetched through a request, the light or dark mode option of a UI, and a list of errors that you got from filling a form in the UI are all examples of what can be state.

Let's look at the following example:

```
const NotState = ({aList = [1, 2, 3, 4, 5, 6, 7, 8, 9, 10
  ]}) => {
  const value = "a constant value";
  const filteredList = aList.filter((item) => item % 2 ===
    0);

  return filteredList.map((item) =>
    <div key={item}>{item}</div>);
};
```

Here, we have a component called `NotState`. Let's look at the values we have in there and use our rule of thumb.

The `aList` variable is a component prop. Since our component will receive this, it doesn't need to be state.

Our `value` variable is assigned a string value. Since this value will always be *constant*, then it doesn't need to be state.

Finally, the `filteredList` variable is something that can be derived from our `aList` prop; therefore, it doesn't need to be state.

Now that you are familiar with the concept of state, let's get our hands dirty and understand how can we manage it in React.

Managing state in React

Before diving into some examples, it is important to mention that in this book, *all the examples shown are in a React version after 16.8*. This is because **React Hooks** were introduced in this version. Hooks changed the way we write React code and allowed for the appearance of libraries such as React Query, so it makes sense that any examples shown leverage them.

> **What is React Query?**
> React Query is a protocol-agnostic collection of hooks for fetching, caching, and updating server state in React.

In this section, I'll show you how React allows us to handle state in a component and what we should do if we need to share state between components.

Let's consider the following scenario.

I want to build an application that allows me to count something. In this application, I want to be able to do the following:

- See the current counter value
- Increment my counter
- Decrement my counter
- Reset the counter

Let's imagine that we have a React component called `App`:

```jsx
const App = () => {
  ...

  return (
    <div className="App">
      <div>Counter: {count}</div>
      <div>
        <button onClick={increment}>+1</button>
        <button onClick={decrement}>-1</button>
        <button onClick={reset}>Reset</button>
      </div>
    </div>
```

This app provides the UI needed to handle our counter needs, such as a `div` that we should use to display our `count` and three buttons with an `onClick` event waiting for a callback function to perform each of the following actions needed.

We are just missing the heart of this component, which is the state. Natively, React gives us two ways to hold state in our applications: `useState` and `useReducer`.

Let's start by looking at `useState`.

Managing state with useState

`useState` is a React Hook that allows you to hold a stateful value. When calling this hook, it will return the stateful value and a function to update it.

Let's look at an example of how to leverage `useState` to build the counter application:

```
const App = () => {
  const [count, setCount] = useState(0);

  const increment = () => setCount((currentCount) =>
    currentCount + 1);
  const decrement = () => setCount((currentCount) =>
    currentCount - 1);
  const reset = () => setCount(0);

  return (
    <div className="App">
      <div>Counter: {count}</div>
      <div>
        <button onClick={increment}>+1</button>
        <button onClick={decrement}>-1</button>
        <button onClick={reset}>Reset</button>
      </div>
    </div>
  );
};
```

The preceding snippet leverages the `useState` hook to hold our counter state. When we first call `useState`, two things are done:

- The state value is initiated as 0
- The `count` state variable is destructured; then, the same is done to the state updater function, called `setCount`

After this, we declare functions where we use the state updater function, `setCount`, to either increment, decrement, or reset our state variable.

Finally, we assign our state variable to the respective UI section and pass the callbacks to our buttons' `onClick` events.

With that, we have built a simple counter application. Our application will start rendering our count as 0. Every time we click on the buttons, it will execute the respective state update, re-render our application, and display the new count value.

`useState` is the answer most of the time when you need any state in your React applications. Just don't forget to apply the "*what will I store in my state?*" rule of thumb before!

Now, let's see an example of how to manage state and build the same counter application by using the `useReducer` hook.

Managing state with useReducer

`useReducer` is the preferred option when we have a more complex state. Before using the hook, we need to do some setup so that we have everything we need to send to our `useReducer` hook:

```
const initialState = { count: 0 };

const types = {
  INCREMENT: "increment",
  DECREMENT: "decrement",
  RESET: "reset",
};

const reducer = (state, action) => {
  switch (action) {
    case types.INCREMENT:
      return { count: state.count + 1 };
    case types.DECREMENT:
      return { count: state.count - 1 };
    case types.RESET:
      return { count: 0 };
    default:
      throw new Error("This type does not exist");
  }
};
```

In the preceding snippet, we created three things:

- An `initialState` object. This object has a property count with 0 as its value.
- A `types` object that describes all the action types we will support.
- A **reducer**. This reducer is responsible for receiving our state and action. By matching that action with the expected type, we'll be able to update the state.

Now that the setup is done, let's create our counter:

```
const AppWithReducer = () => {
  const [state, dispatch] = useReducer(reducer,
    initialState);

  const increment = () => dispatch(types.INCREMENT);
  const decrement = () => dispatch(types.DECREMENT);
  const reset = () => dispatch(types.RESET);

  return (
    <div className="App">
      <div>Counter: {state.count}</div>
      <div>
        <button onClick={increment}>+1</button>
        <button onClick={decrement}>-1</button>
        <button onClick={reset}>Reset</button>
      </div>
    </div>
  );
};
```

The preceding snippet leverages the `useReducer` hook to hold our counter state. When we first call `useReducer`, three things are done:

- We indicate to our hook what `reducer` should be used
- We initialize our state with the `initialState` object
- We destructure the `state` object and then the `dispatch` function, which allows us to dispatch an action from the `useReducer` hook

After this, we create the functions that will be responsible for calling the `dispatch` function with the expected action.

Finally, we assign our state variable to the respective UI section and pass the callbacks to our buttons' `onClick` events.

With these two *hooks* under your belt, you now know how to manage state in your components.

Now, let's picture the following scenario: what if you need your counter state to be accessible in other components?

You could pass them by props. But what if this state needs to be sent to five other components and different levels on the tree? Would you be prop-drilling it and passing it to every component?

To deal with this scenario and improve your code readability, **React Context** was created.

Sharing state with React Context

Context allows you to natively share values between components without having to prop drill them. Let's learn how to build a context to handle our counter:

```
import { useState, createContext } from "react";

export const CountContext = createContext();

export const CountStore = () => {
  const [count, setCount] = useState(0);

  const increment = () => setCount((currentCount) =>
    currentCount + 1);
  const decrement = () => setCount((currentCount) =>
    currentCount - 1);
  const reset = () => setCount(0);

  return {
    count,
    increment,
    decrement,
    reset,
  };
};

const CountProvider = (children) => {
  return <CountContext.Provider value={CountStore()}
    {...children} />;
};

export default CountProvider;
```

In the preceding snippet, we are doing three things:

- Using the `createContext` function to create our context.
- Creating a **store**. This store will be responsible for holding our state. Here, you can see we leverage the `useState` hook. At the end of the store, we return an object that contains the functions to do the state updates and create our state variable.
- Creating a `CountProvider`. This provider is responsible for creating a provider that will be used to wrap a component. This will allow every component that is inside of that provider to access our `CountStore` values.

Once this setup has been done, we need to make sure our components can access our context:

```
root.render(
  <CountProvider>
    <App />
  </CountProvider>
);
```

The preceding snippet leverages `CountProvider`, which we created in the *previous snippet*, to wrap up our App component. This allows every component inside App to consume our context:

```
import { CountContext } from "./CountContext/CountContext";

const AppWithContext = () => {
  const { count, increment, decrement, reset } =
    useContext(CountContext);

  return (
    <div className="App">
      <div>Counter: {count}</div>
      <div>
        <button onClick={increment}>+1</button>
        <button onClick={decrement}>-1</button>
        <button onClick={reset}>Reset</button>
      </div>
    </div>
  );
};
```

Finally, in this snippet, we leverage the `useContext` hook to consume our `CountContext`. Since our component is rendered inside our custom provider, we can access the state held inside our context.

Every time the state updates inside of our context, React will make sure that every component that is consuming our context will re-render, as well as receive the state updates. This can often lead to unnecessary re-renders because if you are consuming only a variable from the state and for some reason another variable changes, then the context will force all consumers to re-render.

One of the downsides of context is that often, unrelated logic tends to get grouped. As you can see from the preceding snippets, it comes at the cost of a bit of boilerplate code.

Now, Context is still great, and it's how React enables you to share state between components. However, it was not always around, so the community had to come up with ideas on how to enable state sharing. To do so, state management libraries were created.

What do different state management libraries have in common?

One of the freedoms React offers you is that it does not impose any standards or practices for your development. While this is great, it also leads to different practices and implementations.

To make this easier and give developers some structure, state management libraries were created:

- **Redux** promotes an approach focused on stores, reducers, and selectors. This leads to needing to learn specific concepts and filling your project with a bunch of boilerplate code that might impact the code's readability and increase code complexity.
- **Zustand** promotes a custom hook approach where each hook holds your state. This is by far the simplest solution and currently my favorite one. It synergizes with React and fully embraces hooks.
- **MobX** doesn't impose an architecture but focuses on a functional reactive approach. This leads to more specific concepts, and the diversity of practices can lead the developer to run into the same struggles of code structure that they might already suffer from with React.

One common thing in all these libraries is that all of them are trying to solve the same type of issues that we tried to solve with React Context: *a way to manage our shared state*.

The state that is accessible to multiple components inside a React tree is often called global state. Now, global state is often misunderstood, which leads to the addition of unnecessary complexity to your code and often needing to resort to the libraries mentioned in this section.

At the end of the day, each developer and team have their preferences and choices. Considering React gives you the freedom to handle your state however you want, you must consider all the advantages and disadvantages of each solution before making your choice. Migrating from one to another can take a lot of time and completely change the paradigm of how state is handled in your application, so choose wisely and take your time.

While global state is not the reason why React Query was built, it has an impact on its creation. The way global state is often composed led to the need to manage a specific part of it that has many challenges. This specific part is called server state and the way it was historically handled paved the way to motivate Tanner Linsley to create React Query.

Summary

In this chapter, we became familiar with the concept of state. By now, you should understand the importance of state as the heart of React applications and know how you can manage it natively with the help of `useState` and `useReducer`.

You learned that sometimes, you need to share your state with multiple components and that you can do it with Context or by leveraging a third-party state management library. Each of these solutions has its pros and cons, and at the end of the day, it will be a question of developer preference.

In *Chapter 2*, *Server State versus Client State*, you will understand more about global state, and you find out that often, our global state is a combination of both server and client state. You will learn what these terms mean, how to identify these states, and what the common challenges associated with them are.

2
Server State versus Client State

Global state is the most common way we look at state. It is the state that is shared globally in our application by one or more components.

What we don't often know is that in our day-to-day development, our global state ends up being split between the state that persists outside of our application and the state that only exists within our application. The first type of state is called **server state**, while the second one is called **client state**. Both of these types of states have their specific challenges and require different tools to help manage them.

In this chapter, we will understand why we refer mostly to our state as global state and why we should adjust our mental models to include client and server states instead.

We'll also review what each type of state is responsible for and how to differentiate them in an application and understand the challenges that led to the creation of React Query.

By the end of this chapter, you'll be able to fully split global state into the client state and the server state by applying the mental models you will have just learned.

You will also understand all the challenges created by having a server state in your application and prepare to overcome them with React Query.

In this chapter, we'll be covering the following topics:

- What is global state?
- What is client state?
- What is server state?
- Understanding common challenges with server state

Technical requirements

All the code examples for this chapter can be found on GitHub at `https://github.com/PacktPublishing/State-management-with-React-Query/tree/feat/chapter_2`.

What is global state?

When starting with state management in the React world, we are often not familiar with the different concepts of state.

Often, we just look at state by thinking about the amount of `useState` or `useReducer` hooks we have in our components. Then, when the `useState` or `useReducer` pattern stops working and we need to share state between more components, we either lift our state to the nearest parent when this state is needed only by the children of that component, or find a common place where this state can exist and be accessible everywhere by all the components we want. This state is often called global state.

Let's look at an example of what global state can look like in an application. Here, we have a store responsible for managing theme selection, fetching data, and tracking the loading state of this fetching request:

```
const theme = {
  DARK: "dark",
  LIGHT: "light",
};

export const GlobalStore = () => {
  const [selectedTheme, setSelectedTheme] = useState
    (theme.LIGHT);
  const [serverData, setServerData] = useState(null);
  const [isLoadingData, setIsLoadingData] = useState
    (false);

  const toggleTheme = () => {
    setSelectedTheme((currentTheme) =>
      currentTheme === theme.LIGHT ? theme.DARK :
        theme.LIGHT
    );
  };

  const fetchData = (name = "Daniel") => {
```

```
      setIsLoadingData(true);
      fetch(`<insert_url_here>/${name}`)
        .then((response) => response.json())
        .then((responseData) => {
          setServerData(responseData);
        })
   .finally(() => {
        setIsLoadingData(false);
      })
        .catch(() => setIsLoadingData(false));
  };

  useEffect(() => {
    fetchData();
  }, []);

  return {
    selectedTheme,
    toggleTheme,
    serverData,
    isLoadingData,
    fetchData
  };
};
```

This snippet shows an example of what some typical global state can look like. By using React Context, we are creating a store that has the following things inside it:

- A state variable called `selectedTheme` to manage the selected theme
- A state variable called `serverData` to display the data that was returned from our API request
- A state variable called `isLoadingData` to display whether the current loading state of our API request is still loading
- A function called `toggleTheme` to allow us to toggle between light and dark modes
- A `fetchData` function to allow us to fetch the given data and set our loading state as `true` or `false` depending on the state of the request
- A `useEffect` hook that will trigger the initial data fetching to provision our `serverData` state

> **What is useEffect?**
> `useEffect` is a React hook that allows you to perform side effects in your components.

All these are returned from our store so that the consumers of this context can access them from all over our application as long as they subscribe to our context.

Now, from a first look, there seems to be nothing wrong with this state, and it might be enough for most applications. The thing is, most of the time, this state will end up growing due to new development needs. This will lead to increasing the size of our state most of the time.

Let's now picture that we need a secondary theme, and we need to add another state variable called `secondaryTheme`. Our code would look a lot like this:

```
const [selectedTheme, setSelectedTheme] = useState(theme.
LIGHT);
const [secondaryTheme, setSecondaryTheme] = useState(theme.
LIGHT);
...
  const toggleSecondaryTheme = () => {
    setSecondaryTheme((currentTheme) =>
      currentTheme === theme.LIGHT ? theme.DARK :
        theme.LIGHT
    );
  };

  const toggleTheme = () => {
    setSelectedTheme((currentTheme) =>
      currentTheme === theme.LIGHT ? theme.DARK :
        theme.LIGHT
    );
  };
```

So, in this snippet, we added our `secondaryTheme` state variable, and it works very much like `selectedTheme`.

Now, we are using context here; this means that every time we trigger a state update, any component that consumes this state will be forced to re-render to receive the new state updates. What does this mean to us?

Let's imagine we have two components (let's call them *Component A* and *Component B*) consuming this context, but *Component B* only destructures the `selectedTheme` state while *Component A* destructures everything. If *Component A* triggers a state update on `secondaryTheme`, then *Component B* will also re-render because React noticed an update inside the context that both of them share.

This is how React Context works, and we can't change this. We could argue that we could either split the context, split the subscribing component into two components and wrap the second one with `memo`, or just wrap our return with the `useMemo` hook. Sure, this would probably fix our issue, but we are only dealing with the changes in one type of state that creates the global state.

> **What are memo and useMemo?**
>
> `memo` is a function that you can wrap your component in to define a memoized version of it. This will guarantee that your component doesn't re-render unless its props have changed.
>
> `useMemo` is a React hook that allows you to memoize a value. Usually, the value we want to memoize is the result of an expensive calculation.

Now, imagine we needed to add another API request context. Once again, the context grows and we end up with the same issue we had with the themes.

As you may already understand by now, state organization can be a nightmare sometimes. We could resort to a third-party library to help us with this but, once again, this is only a small part of our issues with our state.

So far, we have only been dealing with the organization of state, but now imagine we need to cache the data that we got from our API request. This can lead us to madness.

From these issues we have just noticed, we can see that inside our global state, we tend to have different challenges, and a solution that works for one thing might not work for another. This is why it is important to split our global state. Our global state is often a mix between client state and server state. In the upcoming sections, you will understand what each one of these states is, and we'll focus on server state to finally understand why React Query has become so popular and made our lives so much easier as a developer.

What is client state?

I know, by now, you must be thinking, when is this book going to start React Querying? We are almost there, I promise you. I just need you to fully understand why I love React Query so much and to do so, it is important to understand the main problem it solves.

Now, client state is not one of the problems it solves, but you must be able to identify client state in your day-to-day life as a developer so that you fully understand what should be managed by React Query and what should be managed by other state management tools.

Client state is the state that is owned by your application.

Here are a couple of things that help define your client state:

- This state is synchronous, which means you can access it without any waiting time and by using synchronous APIs.
- It is local; therefore, it only exists in your application.
- It is temporary, so it may get lost upon a page reload and is generally non-persistent between sessions.

With this knowledge in mind, if you were to look back at `GlobalStore`, what would you identify as belonging to client state?

Probably only `selectedTheme`, right?

Let us apply our learning from the previous bullet points:

- Do we need to wait to get its value? *No*, so that means it is synchronous.
- Does the `selectedTheme` only exist in our application? *Yes*.
- Will it be lost on a page reload? *Yes*, if we don't persist it in local storage or check the browser preferences, then its value will be lost between page reloads.

With this in mind, we can definitely say that `selectedTheme` belongs in our client state.

To manage this type of state, we can use anything from React Context to third-party libraries such as Redux, Zustand, or MobX when things start to become harder to organize and maintain.

If we ask the same questions for our `serverData` state variable, would it work the same?

- Does the data only exist in our application? *No*, it exists on a database somewhere.
- Will it be lost on page reload? *No*, the database still keeps the data, so when we reload, it will be fetched once again.
- Do we need to wait to get it? *Yes*, we need to trigger a fetching request to get this data.

This means that our `serverData` state variable doesn't belong in our client state. This is something that we would classify as part of server state.

Let us now get into the thing that brought you to this book and made React Query necessary.

What is server state?

We have always had server state in our applications. The main issue was that we tried to tie it in with our client state management solutions. A common example of trying to tie our server state with our client state management solutions is using either **Redux Saga** or **Redux Thunk**. Both of them made it easier to do data fetching and store your server state. The main issue starts when we have to deal with some of the challenges server state brings us, but let's not get ahead of ourselves; you will understand these challenges in the next section.

Now, what is server state, you might be wondering?

Well, as the name says, server state is the type of state that is stored on your server. Here are a couple of things that help identify your server state:

- This state is asynchronous, which means you need to use asynchronous APIs for fetching and updating it.
- It is persisted remotely – most of the time on a database or external place you don't own or control.
- There are no guarantees that this state is up to date in your application because most often, you have shared ownership of it, and it might be changed by others that are consuming it as well.

With this knowledge in mind, let us look back at `GlobalStore` and our `serverData` state variable and apply these rules to identify our server state:

- Do we need asynchronous APIs to access this state? We do! We need to send a fetch request to the server and wait for it to send the data back.
- Is it persisted remotely? It sure is. Like I just said in the previous bullet item, we need to ask our server for it.
- Will this state always be up to date in our application? We don't know. We don't control the state. This means that if anyone that is consuming the same API decides to update it, then our `serverData` state variable will immediately be outdated.

Now, you might be looking back at `GlobalStore` and asking the following: if `selectedTheme` is client state and `data` is server state, then what is the `isLoadingData` state variable?

Well, this is a derived state variable. This means that its state will always depend on the current status of our `serverData` fetching request. If we fetch data, then `isLoadingData` will be `true`; once we are done fetching data, then `isLoadingData` will go back to `false`.

Now, imagine needing one of these derived state variables for every type of server state variable you have in your application. I'm also going to ask you to picture a scenario in which you needed to handle errors when a fetch request fails. You would probably create another state variable for errors, right? But wouldn't you end up with the same issue as your loading state?

The previously mentioned scenario is just the very small tip of the iceberg of challenges that the server state brings to your application. Imagine that one of your team technical leads arrives at the office one day and tells you that now you need to start caching your data; oh God, another challenge that we didn't think about. As you can see, the server state has many challenges, and in the next section, we will see a couple of them.

Understanding common challenges with server state

By now, you have probably figured out that the server state comes with quite its fair share of challenges. These challenges made React Query stand out even more when it came out because it solved them in such a simple way for developers that it seemed too good to be true.

Now, what are these challenges, and why are they so complex to solve most of the time?

In this section, we will see all the common challenges that we have with the server state and understand a bit of the hard work we had to do as developers to solve them ourselves before we had React Query.

Caching

This is probably one of the hardest challenges we face in server state management.

To improve your page performance and make your site more responsive, very often, you will need to cache your data. This means being able to reuse data that you previously fetched to avoid refetching it from the server once again.

Now, you might be thinking that this sounds simple, but consider the following things:

- While keeping your application responsive, you need to update your cache in the background.
- You need to be able to evaluate when your cache data has become stale and needs to be updated.
- Once data has not been accessed for a while, you must garbage-collect this data.
- You might want to initialize your cache with some template data before data is fetched.

As you can see, caching comes with its fair share of issues, and imagine having to solve all of these by yourself.

Optimistic updates

When performing mutations, you often want to make your user experience better. A mutation is a request that will either create or update your server state. Sometimes, you want to make your user experience better. We all hate filling out a form and ending up watching a loading spinner while our application in the background performs the mutation, refetches the data, and updates the UI.

To make the user experience better, we can resort to optimistic updates.

An optimistic update is when during an ongoing mutation, we update our UI to show how it will look after that mutation is complete, although that mutation is still not confirmed as complete. Basically, we are optimistic that this data will change and be what we are expecting it to be after the mutation, so we save our users some time and give them a UI that they will end up seeing earlier.

Now, imagine implementing this. While doing a mutation, you would need to update the server state in your application with the way we expect it to be after the mutation is successful. This would make the UI more responsive for the user and they can start interacting with it earlier. After the mutation is successful, you need to retrigger a manual refetch for the server state so that you actually have the updated state in your application. Now, picture a scenario in which the mutation fails. You would need to manually roll back your state to the previous version before your optimistic update.

Optimistic updates give an amazing user experience to your users but having to manage all the success and error scenarios, plus keeping your server date updated, can be a hard thing to do.

Deduping requests

Let's paint the following scenario.

You have a button in your UI that, when clicked on by the user, triggers a fetch request to partially update your server state. When the fetch is being performed, the button is disabled.

This might seem okay and not troublesome at all but imagine that before your loading state updates and your button ends up being disabled, the user can click on the button 10 more times. What do you get? Ten more unexpected requests for the same data in your application.

This is why deduping requests is important. When fetching for the exact same type of data, if we trigger multiple requests for the same data, we want only one of those requests to be sent and avoid polluting our user network with unnecessary requests.

Now, imagine having to implement this by yourself. You would need to be aware of all the requests currently being done in your application. When one of those requests exactly matches another one, then you would need to cancel that second, third, or fourth request.

Performance optimization

Sometimes, you need some extra performance optimization in your server state. Here are some common patterns that you might need for specific optimization of your server state management.

- **Lazy loading**: You might only want a specific data fetching request to be done once a certain condition is met.
- **Infinite scrolling**: When dealing with huge lists, infinite scrolling is a very common pattern where you just progressively load more data into your server state.
- **Paginated data**: To help structure large datasets, you can opt to paginate your data. This means that whenever a user decides to move from page 1 to page 2, you will need to fetch the corresponding data for this page.

As you can see, there are several challenges that we need to solve in order to have what we can consider the best experience dealing with server state in our application.

The issue is that deciding to take care of these challenges ourselves as developers can take quite a while, and the code we end up creating is often prone to bugs. Most of the time, these implementations end up affecting a lot of our code readability and significantly increasing the complexity it takes to understand our projects.

What if I told you that there was something that could take care of all of these challenges and many others in the background for you while giving you a super-clean and simple API that will make your code more readable, easier to understand, and make you feel like a true master of server state?

If you are reading this book, then you probably already know the answer. Yes, I'm talking about React Query.

So, pack up your server state knowledge, and prepare your projects because starting with the next chapter, we will change the way you handle server state.

Summary

In this chapter, we fully understood the concept of global state. By now, you should be able to understand why often our state is called global state and how much harder it can be to maintain it if we don't split it.

You learned how to split your state into client and server states and understand how each of these types of states is important for your application and how you can identify them in your code.

Finally, you were familiarized with the challenges that server state can bring to your application and understood that if you were to address them all by yourself, then your code complexity would increase significantly and you'd probably lose some much-needed sleeping hours.

In *Chapter 3, React Query – Introducing, Installing, and Configuring It*, you will start getting hands-on with React Query. You will understand what it is and how it saves you from all the headaches that server state brings to your applications. You will learn how to install and configure it for your application and how you can add dedicated React Query developer tools to make your life even easier as a developer.

3
React Query – Introducing, Installing, and Configuring It

React Query is a library created to make it easier for React developers to manage their server state. It makes it easier for developers to overcome all the challenges that come with server state while making their applications faster, easier to maintain, and reducing many lines in their code.

In this chapter, you will be introduced to React Query and understand why it was created.

You will also get to know the main concepts of React Query – **queries** and **mutations**.

Once you have been introduced to React Query, we'll install it in our application and identify the initial configurations we need to make in our code to get ready to use it fully.

By the end of this chapter, you will know all about React Query Devtools so that you can have a better developer experience while using React Query.

In this chapter, we'll be covering the following topics:

- What is React Query?
- Installing React Query
- Configuring React Query
- Adding React Query Devtools to your application

Technical requirements

In this chapter, we will add React Query v4 to our application. To do so, there are a couple of things we need:

- Your browser needs to be compatible with the following configurations:
  - The Google Chrome version needs to be at least version 73
  - The Mozilla Firefox version needs to be at least version 78
  - The Microsoft Edge version needs to be at least version 79
  - The Safari version needs to be at least version 12.0
  - The Opera version needs to be at least version 53
- A React project after version 16.8

All the code examples for this chapter can be found on GitHub at `https://github.com/PacktPublishing/State-management-with-React-Query/tree/feat/chapter_3`

What is React Query?

React Query is a protocol-agnostic collection of hooks for fetching, caching, and updating server state in React.

It was created by Tanner Linsley and is part of a collection of open source libraries called TanStack.

By default, React Query can also work with React Native out of the box, and it is written in TypeScript so that you can benefit from all its advantages, such as type narrowing and type inference.

Since version 4, React Query has been embedded in a collection of libraries called TanStack Query. TanStack Query made it possible to propagate all the amazing features of React Query to other frameworks and libraries, such as Vue, Solid, and Svelte.

React Query leverages queries and mutations to handle your server state. Upon reading this last sentence, you might wonder what queries and mutations are. I'll show you some code in subsequent chapters so that you can see how React Query handles them, but first, let us learn about queries and mutations.

Query

A query is a request you make to an asynchronous source to fetch your data. Queries can be performed in React Query as long as you have a function that triggers the data-fetching request.

By allowing us to wrap our requests inside of promise-returning functions, React Query supports REST, GraphQL, and any other asynchronous data-fetching clients.

In React Query, the `useQuery` custom hook allows you to subscribe to queries.

Mutation

A mutation is an operation that allows you to create, update, or delete your server state.

Like queries, as long as you have a function that triggers a mutation, React Query supports REST, GraphQL, and any other asynchronous data-fetching clients.

In React Query, the `useMutation` custom hook allows you to perform a mutation.

How does React Query solve my server state challenges?

What if I told you that all the challenges presented in the previous chapter could be solved by React Query?

Out of the box and with zero configurations, React Query supports all the following amazing features:

- **Caching**: After each query, data will be cached during a configurable time and can be reused throughout your application.
- **Query cancelation**: Your queries can be canceled, and you can perform an action after this cancelation.
- **Optimistic updates**: During a mutation, you can easily update your state so that you can provide a better user experience to your users. You are also able to easily revert to a previous state if the mutation fails.
- **Parallel queries**: If you need to execute one or more queries simultaneously, you can do so without any difficulty or impacting your cache.
- **Dependent queries**: Sometimes, we need to execute a query after another one finishes. React Query makes this simple and avoids chaining promises.
- **Paginated queries**: This UI pattern is made easier with React Query. You'll find that using a paginated API, changing pages, and rendering the fetched data is super simple.
- **Infinite queries**: Another UI pattern that is made easier by React Query. You can implement infinite scrolls into your UI and trust React Query to make your life easier when fetching data.
- **Scroll restoration**: Have you ever navigated from a page and, when navigated back, found that the page was scrolled to the exact point where you were before you navigated away? This is scroll restoration, and as long as your query results are cached, it will work out of the box.
- **Data refetching**: Need to trigger a refetch for your data? React Query allows you to do this with pretty much a line of code.

- **Data prefetching**: Sometimes, you can identify ahead of time what the needs and next actions of your users are. When this happens, you can trust React Query to help you prefetch that data ahead of time and cache it for you. This way, your user experience will be improved, and you will have happier users.
- **Tracking network mode and offline support**: Have you ever had to deal with scenarios where your user lost their internet connection while using your application? Well, don't worry because React Query can track the current state of your network, and if a query fails because the user lost connection, it will be retried once the network returns.

Looking at this list is amazing, right?

Just having caching out of the box is a super, great timesaver because it is definitely one of the hardest things to implement when dealing with server state.

Before React Query, it was much harder to handle the server state in our applications. We tried, but our solutions ended up growing more complex and with less maintainable code. Often, these implementations would even end up impacting the user experience because our applications would get less responsive.

With React Query, you are now able to greatly reduce the number of lines in your code, make your application much easier to read and simple, and at the same time, make your application faster and much more responsive.

I won't get into more technical details right now because, hopefully, in the following chapters, you will see all these features working and start understanding why React Query makes your life so much easier.

For now, let us start by installing React Query in our applications.

Installing React Query

Now that you are aware of React Query, you are probably thinking, *wow, I really need to add this to my project*. Wait no more – here is what you need to do to install React Query.

Depending on your project type, you can install React Query in several ways.

npm

If you are running npm in your project, then this is what you need to do to install React Query.

In your terminal, run the following command:

```
npm i @tanstack/react-query
```

Yarn

If Yarn is what you prefer, then this is what you need to do to install React Query.

In your terminal, run the following command:

```
yarn add @tanstack/react-query
```

pnpm

If you are a fan of a new package manager, such as pnpm, and are using it in your project, then this is what you need to do to install React Query.

In your terminal, run the following command:

```
pnpm add @tanstack/react-query
```

Script tag

Not using a package manager? Don't worry, because React Query can be added to your application by using a global build that is hosted on a **content delivery network**.

> **Content delivery network (CDN)**
> A CDN is a geographically distributed group of servers that work together to allow for faster delivery of content on the internet.

To add React Query to your application, add the next `script` tag at the end of your HTML file:

```
<script src="https://unpkg.com/@tanstack/react-query@4/build/umd/index.production.js"></script>
```

You should now have React Query installed in your project.

Now, we need to do the initial configurations on our projects to be able to use all the core functionalities of React Query.

Configuring React Query

React Query has a very fast and simple configuration. This improves the developer experience and can prepare you to start migrating your server state to React Query as soon as possible.

To add React Query to your application, there are only two things you need to know:

- **QueryClient**
- **QueryClientProvider**

QueryClient

As you should be aware right now, caching is one of the most important things React Query makes easier for developers. In React Query, there are two mechanisms used to handle this cache called **QueryCache** and **MutationCache**.

`QueryCache` is responsible for storing all the data related to your queries. This can be the data of your query as well as its current state.

`MutationCache` is responsible for storing all the data related to your mutations. This can be the data of your mutation as well as its current state.

To make it easier for a developer to abstract from both caches, React Query created `QueryClient`. This is responsible for being the interface between a developer and a cache.

The first thing you should do when setting your application with React Query is to create a `QueryClient` instance. To do so, you need to import it from the `@tanstack/react-query` package and instantiate it:

```
import {
  QueryClient,
} from '@tanstack/react-query'
const queryClient = new QueryClient()
```

In the preceding snippet, we create a new `QueryClient` object. As we don't pass any argument when instantiating the object, `QueryClient` will assume all the defaults.

There are four options we can send as arguments when creating our `QueryClient`. They are as follows:

- `queryCache`: The query cache that this client will use throughout our application.
- `mutationCache`: The mutation cache that this client will use throughout our application.
- `logger`: The logger that this client will use to display errors, warnings, and useful information for debugging. When nothing is specified, then React Query will use the console object.
- `defaultOptions`: The default options that all queries and mutations will use throughout our application.

Now, you might be wondering when you should manually set each one of these arguments instead of using the default ones. The following subsections will tell you when.

QueryCache and MutationCache

Here is a small spoiler that hopefully you will review and understand better in the following chapters, but it is essential to understand when you should manually configure either `QueryCache` or `MutationCache` – all queries and mutations can execute some code whenever there is an error, or when its execution succeeds. This code is represented by the `onSuccess` and `onError` functions. Also, in the case of mutations, you can also execute some code before the mutation executes. In this scenario, the function that represents this is called `onMutate`.

In the case of `QueryCache`, this is how it would look:

```
import { QueryCache } from '@tanstack/react-query'
const queryCache = new QueryCache({
  onError: error => {
    // do something on error
  },
  onSuccess: data => {
    // do something on success
  }
})
```

Before explaining the preceding snippet, let's look at the very similar `MutationCache`:

```
import { MutationCache } from '@tanstack/react-query'

const mutationCache = new MutationCache({
  onError: error => {
    // do something on error
  },
  onSuccess: data => {
    // do something on success
  },
  onMutate: newData => {
    // do something before the mutation
  },
})
```

As you can see, both snippets are similar, except for the `onMutate` function on `MutationCache`.

By default, these functions don't have any behavior, but if, for some reason, you intend on always doing something whenever you perform a mutation or a query, then you can do this configuration inside the respective function of the respective object when instantiating the cache object.

Then, you can send this object to `QueryClient` when instantiating it:

```
const queryClient = new QueryClient({
  mutationCache,
  queryCache
})
```

In the preceding snippet, we instantiated a new `QueryClient` with our custom `MutationCache` and `QueryCache` functions.

Logger

Are you using `logger` outside of the `console` object in your project? Then, you might want to configure it in your `QueryClient`.

Here is what you need to do:

```
const logger = {
    log: (...args) => {
        // here you call your custom log function
    },
    warn: (...args) => {
        // here you call your custom warn function
    },
    error: (...args) => {
        // here you call your custom error function
    },
};
```

In the preceding snippet, we created a `logger` object. This object has three functions that React Query will call whenever it needs to `log` an error, `warn` about an error, or display `error`. You can override these functions and add your custom logger.

Then, all you need to do is pass this `logger` object to your `QueryClient` when instantiating it:

```
const queryClient = new QueryClient({
  logger
})
```

In the preceding snippet, we instantiated a new `QueryClient` with our custom logger.

defaultOptions

There are options that are used as defaults for all the mutations or queries that you execute throughout your application. `defaultOptions` allows you to override these defaults. There are many defaults, and I'll avoid showing all of them to avoid spoilers for the next chapters, but don't worry – I'll do a callback to these options when the right time arrives.

Here is how you override your `defaultOptions`:

```
const defaultOptions = {
  queries: {
    staleTime: Infinity,
  },
};
```

What we did in the preceding snippet was create a `defaultOptions` object and, inside it, a `queries` object. Inside this `queries` object, we specified that `staleTime` for all queries will be `Infinity`. Once again, don't worry about not having a definition for this yet. You will understand it in the next chapter.

Once this setup is done, all you need to do is pass this `defaultOptions` object to your `QueryClient` when instantiating it, and all the queries will have the `staleTime` property set to `Infinity`.

Here is how to do it:

```
const queryClient = new QueryClient({
  defaultOptions
})
```

In the preceding snippet, we instantiated a new `QueryClient` with our custom `defaultOptions` object.

Okay, so now you are aware of `QueryClient` and should understand its role as the brain of React Query.

So, you might be thinking, considering that React Query is based on hooks for doing the queries and mutations, do we need to always pass our `QueryClient` to all our hooks?

Imagine if this was the case! We all would be sick and tired of all the prop drilling in our application even before we used our second or third hook.

Let us now see the way that React Query saves us some time by introducing `QueryClientProvider`.

QueryClientProvider

To make the process of sharing our `QueryClient` easier for every developer, React Query resorted to something we learned about in *Chapter 1*, and that is React Context. By creating its custom provider called `QueryClientProvider`, React Query allows you to share `QueryClient` with all the custom hooks it provides automatically.

The following snippet shows you how to use React Query's `QueryClientProvider`:

```
import {
  QueryClient,
  QueryClientProvider,
} from '@tanstack/react-query'
// Create a client
const queryClient = new QueryClient()

const App = () => {
  return (
    <QueryClientProvider client={queryClient}>
      <Counter />
    </QueryClientProvider>
  )
}
```

As you can see in the preceding snippet, all you need to do is import your `QueryClientProvider` from the `@tanstack/react-query` package, wrap your main component with it, and pass it to `queryClient` as a prop.

Your application is now ready to start using React Query.

Now, let us see how we can add and use React Query-dedicated developer tools.

Adding React Query Devtools

When debugging our applications, we often find ourselves thinking how amazing it would be to have a way to visualize what is happening inside our application. Well, with React Query, you don't have to worry because it has its own developer tools, or devtools.

React Query Devtools allows you to see and understand the current state of all your queries and mutations. This will save you a lot of time debugging and avoid polluting all your code with unnecessary log functions, even if temporarily.

Depending on the type of project, you can install React Query Devtools in several ways:

- If you are running npm in your project, run the following command:

    ```
    npm i @tanstack/react-query-devtools
    ```

- If you are using Yarn, run the following command:

    ```
    yarn add @tanstack/react-query-devtools
    ```

- If you are using pnpm, run the following command:

    ```
    pnpm add @tanstack/react-query-devtools
    ```

Now, you should have React Query Devtools installed in your application. Let's now see how we can add them to our code.

There are two ways to use Devtools. They are Floating Mode and Embedded Mode.

Floating Mode

Floating Mode will render the React Query logo floating in the corner of your screen. By clicking on it, you can toggle Devtools on or off.

The logo that will show up in the corner of your screen is the following:

Figure 3.1 – The React Query Devtools logo

Once you toggle it, then you will see Devtools:

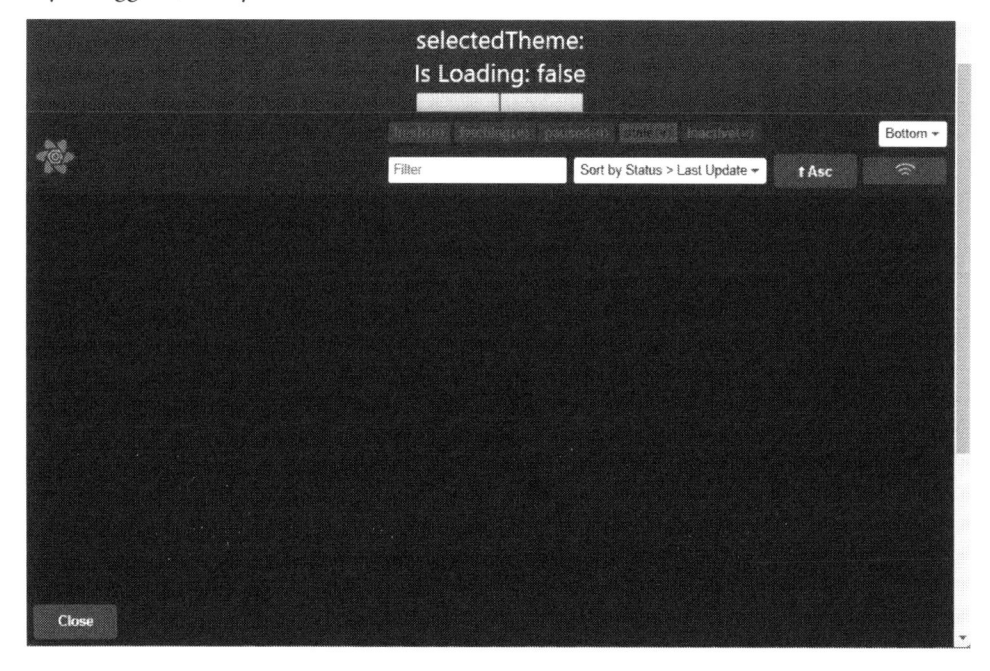

Figure 3.2 – React Query Devtools' Floating Mode

Devtools will be rendered in your **DOM tree** inside a separate HTML element.

Figure 3.3 – React Query Devtools' Floating Mode on the DOM

To add Devtools in Floating Mode to your application, you need to import it:

```
import { ReactQueryDevtools } from '@tanstack/
  react-query-devtools'
```

Once imported, just add it as close to your `QueryClientProvider` as you can:

```
<QueryClientProvider client={queryClient}>
  <ReactQueryDevtools initialIsOpen={false} />
  <Counter />
</QueryClientProvider>
```

Embedded Mode

Embedded Mode will add Devtools embedded as a regular component in your application.

Here is how it looks on your application:

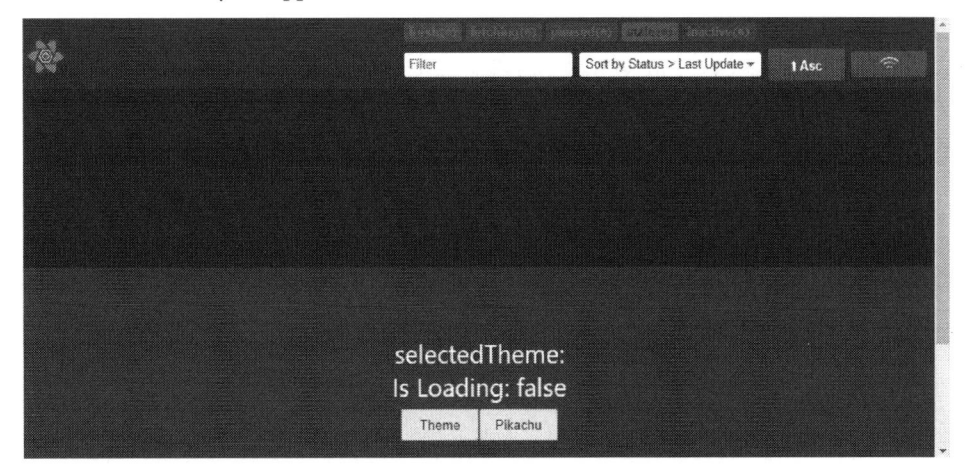

Figure 3.4 – React Query Devtools' Embedded Mode

If you look at your DOM tree, you will see that Devtools is rendered like a regular component.

Figure 3.5 – React Query Devtools' Embedded Mode on the DOM

To use Devtools in Embedded Mode in your application, you need to import it:

```
import { ReactQueryDevtoolsPanel } from '@tanstack/
  react-query-devtools'
```

Once they are imported, just add them as close to your `QueryClientProvider` as possible:

```
<QueryClientProvider client={queryClient}>
  <ReactQueryDevtoolsPanel />
  <Counter />
</QueryClientProvider>
```

By default, Devtools is not included in production builds. Nevertheless, you might want to load them in production to help you debug something. In the next section, we'll see how to do that.

Enabling Devtools in your production build

If you decide to load Devtools in your production environment, you must delay loading it and instead load it dynamically. This is important to help reduce your application bundle size. It is also important to lazy load Devtools because when using our application in production, we might never want to use it, so we want to avoid adding stuff to our build that we will end up not using at all. To lazy load components in React, we can use React.lazy.

Here is how we can import Devtools using React.lazy:

```
const ReactQueryDevtoolsProduction = React.lazy(() =>
  import('@tanstack/react-query-devtools/build/lib/
    index.prod.js').then(
    (d) => ({
      default: d.ReactQueryDevtools,
    }),
  ),
)
```

The preceding snippet wraps a **dynamic import** with React.lazy and assigns the return of the promise to ReactQueryDevtoolsProduction, so that we can lazily load it in our production environment without increasing our bundle size.

> **What is a dynamic import?**
> A dynamic import allows you to load a module from any place in your code asynchronously. This import will return a promise that, when fulfilled, returns an object containing the exports from the module.

The previous snippet should work with all bundlers. If you are using a more modern bundler that supports package exports, then instead you can dynamically import your module like this:

```
const ReactQueryDevtoolsProduction = React.lazy(() =>
  import('@tanstack/react-query-devtools/production').then(
    (d) => ({
      default: d.ReactQueryDevtools,
    }),
```

```
    ),
)
```

In this snippet, we change the path from where we will import our module to one that will work with more modern bundlers.

When using `React.lazy` and trying to render the component we just lazy loaded, React requires that the component should be wrapped with a **Suspense** component. This is important in a scenario where we want to show a fallback while our lazy-loaded component is pending.

> **What is Suspense?**
> `Suspense` allows you to render a loading indication in your UI while the component inside of it is not ready to be rendered yet.

Let us see what we need to do to load our `ReactQueryDevtoolsProduction` component:

```
<React.Suspense fallback={null}>
  <ReactQueryDevtoolsProduction />
</React.Suspense>
```

As you can see in the snippet, we wrap our `ReactQueryDevtoolsProduction` component with `Suspense` so it can be lazy loaded. You can also see that we didn't provide any fallback since what we are trying to load are Devtools, and we don't need to add any pending state while the module is loading.

Now, we don't want to automatically load Devtools whenever we render our component. What we want is a way to toggle them in our application.

Since this is a production build, we don't want to include a button there that might confuse our users. So, a potential way to handle this is by creating a function inside our `window` object called `toggleDevtools`.

This is how the React Query documentation suggests we do it:

```
  const [showDevtools, setShowDevtools] = React.useState
    (false)

  React.useEffect(() => {
    window.toggleDevtools = () => setShowDevtools
      ((previousState) => !previousState)
  }, [])



  return (
```

```
      …
      {showDevtools && (
        <React.Suspense fallback={null}>
          <ReactQueryDevtoolsProduction />
        </React.Suspense>
      )}
      …
  );
```

Here is what we are doing in the preceding snippet:

1. Creating a state variable to hold the current state of the Devtools. This state variable is updated whenever the user toggles the Devtools on or off.
2. Running an effect where we assign the toggle function to our `window`.
3. Inside our return, when our `showDevtools` is toggled on, since we are lazy loading our `ReactQueryDevtoolsProduction` component, we need to wrap it with `Suspense` to be able to render it.

At this point, you have all that you need to start using React Query in your application.

Summary

In this chapter, we learned about TanStack Query and how React Query fits into it. By now, you should be able to identify the primary way React Query makes server state management easier and how it uses queries and mutations.

You learned about `QueryClient` and `QueryClientProvider` and understood how they are fundamental to running React Query in your application. You also learned how you can customize your own `QueryClient` if you need to do so.

Finally, you got to meet the React Query Devtools and learned how to configure it in your project. Also, you are now able to load it into production for those special scenarios when you need to do some extra debugging.

In *Chapter 4*, *Fetching Data with React Query*, you will get to know your best friend for dealing with queries, the `useQuery` custom hook. You'll understand how it works, how to use it, and how it can cache data. You will also learn the ways you can trigger query refetches and how to build dependent queries.

Part 2: Managing Server State with React Query

When dealing with server state, many challenges are attached to how we read from it. From caching to pagination, we will understand how the React Query custom hook called `useQuery` makes this work while giving an amazing combined developer and user experience.

As well as the challenges of how we read our server state, creating, updating, and deleting it brings about another set of challenges. Luckily, React Query has another custom hook that comes to the rescue called `useMutation`.

After understanding the pillars of React Query, you might be wondering whether popular server-side frameworks such as Next.js and Remix allow you to use React Query. Spoiler alert – they do, and you will learn how here.

To wrap up and make sure that you will be able to sleep well at night, you will learn a set of recipes you can use to test your React Query, using components and custom hooks by levering Mock Service Worker and the React Testing Library.

This part includes the following chapters:

- *Chapter 4, Fetching Data with React Query*
- *Chapter 5, More Data-Fetching Challenges*
- *Chapter 6, Performing Data Mutations with React Query*
- *Chapter 7, Server-Side Rendering with Next.js or Remix*
- *Chapter 8, Testing React Query Hooks and Components*

4
Fetching Data with React Query

React Query allows you to fetch, cache, and handle your server state by leveraging one of its custom hooks called `useQuery`. For your data to be cached, React Query has a concept called a query key. In combination with the query keys and a couple of strict defaults, React Query takes your server state management to the next level.

In this chapter, you will be introduced to the `useQuery` hook and understand how React Query allows you to fetch and cache your data. During this process, you will get to know all the defaults that are used in all of your queries. You will also be introduced to some options you can use to make your `useQuery` experience even better.

After becoming familiar with `useQuery`, you can start using it to refetch your queries in certain scenarios. You will also be able to leverage some extra properties of `useQuery` to fetch queries that depend on each other.

At the end of this chapter, we'll review a code file to review what we learned in this chapter.

In this chapter, we'll be covering the following topics:

- What is `useQuery` and how does it work?
- Refetching data with `useQuery`
- Fetching dependent queries with `useQuery`

Technical requirements

All the code examples for this chapter can be found on GitHub at https://github.com/PacktPublishing/State-management-with-React-Query/tree/feat/chapter_4.

What is useQuery and how does it work?

As you learned in the previous chapter, a query is a request you send to an asynchronous source to fetch data.

In the React Query documentation, queries are also defined in the following way:

A query is a declarative dependency on an asynchronous source of data that is tied to a unique key.

(https://tanstack.com/query/v4/docs/guides/queries)

With that concept under your belt, you are now ready to understand how React Query leverages its custom hook, called `useQuery`, to enable you to subscribe to a query.

To use the `useQuery` custom hook, you have to import it like this:

```
import { useQuery } from "@tanstack/react-query";
```

Here is the `useQuery` syntax:

```
const values = useQuery({
    queryKey: <insertQueryKey>,
    queryFn: <insertQueryFunction>,
});
```

As you can see, the `useQuery` hook only needs two parameters for it to work:

- **A query key**: A unique key used to identify your query
- **A query function**: A function that returns a promise

What is a query key?

The query key is a unique value used by React Query to identify your queries. It is also by using the query key that React Query caches your data in `QueryCache`. The query key also allows you to manually interact with the query cache.

The query key needs to be an array that can contain just one string or a bunch of other values, such as objects. All that matters is that the values inside this query key array are serializable.

Before React Query v4, the query key didn't necessarily need to be an array. It could just be a single string because React Query would convert it internally into an array. So, don't find it weird if you find some examples online that don't use an array as a query key.

Here are some valid examples of query keys:

```
useQuery({ queryKey: ['users'] })
useQuery({ queryKey: ['users', 10] })
useQuery({ queryKey: ['users', 10, { isVisible: true }] })
useQuery({ queryKey: ['users', page, filters] })
```

As you can see, so long as it is an array, the query key will be valid.

As good practice and to make your query key more distinct and easier to identify while reading through multiple `useQuery` hooks, you should add all the dependencies of your query as part of the query key. Think of it as the same model of the dependency array you have on your `useEffect` hook. This is helpful for reading purposes as well as because the query key also allows React Query to refetch queries automatically when a dependency of the query changes.

One thing to keep in mind is that the query key is hashed deterministically. This means that the order of the items inside the array matters.

Here are some queries whose query keys, when hashed deterministically, are the same query:

```
useQuery({ queryKey: ['users', 10, { page, filters }] })
useQuery({ queryKey: ['users', 10, { filters, page }] })
useQuery({ queryKey: ['users', 10, { page, random:
  undefined, filters }] })
```

All these examples are the same query – the order of the array in the query key is kept the same throughout the three examples.

Now, you might be wondering how is that possible, considering that the inside of the object page and filters changed place every time, and in the last example, there was a third property called `random`. This is true, but they are still inside an object and that object doesn't change its position inside the query key array. Also, the `random` property is undefined, so when hashing the object, it is excluded.

Now, let's look at some queries whose query keys, when hashed deterministically, are not the same query:

```
useQuery({ queryKey: ['users', 10, undefined, { page,
  filters }] })
useQuery({ queryKey: ['users', { page, filters }, 10] })
useQuery({ queryKey: ['users', 10, { page, filters }] })
```

All these examples represent different queries because when the query key is hashed deterministically, these examples end up being completely different queries. You might be wondering why the first example is not the same as the last one. Shouldn't the `undefined` value disappear as it did from the `{ queryKey: ['users', 10, { page, random: undefined, filters }] })` object?

No, because in this scenario, it's not inside an object, and the order matters. When it's hashed, this undefined value will be transformed into a null value inside the hashed key.

Now that you are familiar with query keys, you can learn more about query functions.

What is a query function?

A query function is a function that returns a promise. This returned promise will either resolve and return the data or throw an error.

As the query function just needs to return a promise, it makes React Query even more powerful because the query function can support any client capable of performing asynchronous data fetching. This means that both **REST** and **GraphQL** are supported, so you can have both options at the same time if you wish.

Now, let's look at an example of a query function that uses GraphQL and another that uses REST:

GraphQL

```
import { useQuery } from "@tanstack/react-query";
import { request, gql } from "graphql-request";

const customQuery = gql`
  query {
    posts {
      data {
        id
        title
      }
    }
  }
`;

const fetchGQL = async () => {
  const endpoint = <add_endpoint_here>
```

```
  const {
    posts: { data },
  } = await request(endpoint, customQuery);
  return data;
};
...
useQuery({
queryKey: ["posts"],
queryFn: fetchGQL
});
```

In the preceding snippet, we can see an example of using React Query with GraphQL. This is what we are doing:

1. We start by creating our GraphQL query and assigning it to our `customQuery` variable.
2. Then, we create the `fetchGQL` function, which will be our query function.
3. In our `useQuery` hook, we pass the respective query key to the hook and our `fetchGQL` function as the query function.

Now, let's see how to do this using REST:

REST

```
import axios from "axios";

const fetchData = async () => {
  const { data } = await axios.get(
    `https://danieljcafonso.builtwithdark.com/
      react-query-api`
  );
  return data;
};
...
useQuery({
    queryKey: ["api"],
    queryFn: fetchData,
  });
```

In the preceding snippet, we can see an example of using React Query with REST. This is what we are doing:

1. We start by creating the `fetchData` function, which will be our query function.
2. In our `useQuery` hook, we pass the respective query key to the hook and our `fetchData` function as the query function.

These examples make React Query shine even more because so long as you have a client that can perform asynchronous data fetching, the client can be used in your query function. As mentioned previously, just so that React Query can handle your error scenarios properly, one thing that we need to check when using these clients is if they automatically throw an error when your request fails. If they do not throw an error, you must throw the error yourself.

This is how you can do this in a query function that uses `fetch`:

```
const fetchDataWithFetch = async () => {
  const response = await fetch('https://danieljcafonso.
    builtwithdark.com/react-query-api')
  if (!response.ok) throw new Error('Something failed in
    your request')
  return response.json()
}
```

In the preceding snippet, after performing a request using `fetch`, we check if our response is valid. If it is not, we throw an error. If everything is OK, we return the response data.

One thing that will eventually pass through your mind as you keep creating queries and building your query functions is that it would be helpful to pass your query key to your query function. After all, if query keys represent the dependencies of your query, then it makes sense that you might need them in your query function.

You can do this, and there are two patterns to do so:

- **Inline function**
- **QueryFunctionContext**

Inline function

When you don't have many parameters in your query key that need to be passed to your query function, you can leverage this pattern. By writing an inline function, you can provide access to the variables in the current scope and pass them to your query function.

Here is an example of this pattern:

```
const fetchData = async (someVariable) => {
  const { data } = await axios.get(
    `https://danieljcafonso.builtwithdark.com/
      react-query-api/${someVariable}`
  );
  return data;
};
...
useQuery({
    queryKey: ["api", someVariable],
    queryFn: () => fetchData(someVariable),
});
```

In the preceding snippet, we start by creating a `fetchData` function that will receive a parameter called `someVariable`. This parameter is then used to complement the URL used to fetch the data. When we get to our `useQuery` declaration, since we need our `someVariable` variable to be used as a dependency of our query, we include it in the query key. Finally, in the query function, we create an inline function that will call `fetchData` with our `someVariable` value.

As you can see, this pattern is great whenever we don't have many parameters. Now, think about the use case where your query key ended up with 12 parameters, and all of them were needed inside of the query function. It's not a bad practice, but it will impact your code readability a bit. To avoid these cases, you can resort to the `QueryFunctionContext` object.

QueryFunctionContext

Every time the query function is called, React Query will take care of automatically passing your query key to the query function as the `QueryFunctionContext` object.

Here is an example of using the `QueryFunctionContext` pattern:

```
const fetchData = async ({ queryKey }) => {
  const [_queryKeyIdentifier, someVariable] = queryKey;
  const { data } = await axios.get(
    `https://danieljcafonso.builtwithdark.com/
      react-query-api/${someVariable}`
  );
  return data;
};
```

```
useQuery({
   queryKey: ["api", someVariable],
   queryFn: fetchData,
});
```

In the preceding snippet, we start by creating our `fetchData` function. This function will be receiving `QueryFunctionContext` as a parameter, so from this object, we can immediately destructure `queryKey`. As you know from the *What is a query key?* section, the query key is an array, so the order in which we passed the parameters we need in our function to our query key matters. In this example, we need the `someVariable` variable, which was passed as the second element of our array, so we destructure our array to get the second element. We then use `someVariable` to complement the URL used to fetch the data. When we get to our `useQuery` declaration, since we need our `someVariable` variable to be used as a dependency of our query, we include it in the query key. As it is included in the query key, it will automatically be sent to our query function.

This pattern reduces the need to create an inline function and enforces the need to add all the dependencies of your query to the query key. The one downside this pattern might have is that with so many parameters, you will have to remember the order you added them to the query key to use them in the query function. One way to fix this issue is by sending an object with all the parameters you need in your query function. This way, you remove the need to remember the order of the elements of your array.

This is how you can do this:

```
useQuery({
   queryKey: [{queryIdentifier: "api", someVariable}],
   queryFn: fetchData,
});
```

By passing an object as your query key, the object will be sent as the `QueryFunctionContext` object to your query function.

Then, in your function, you only need to do this:

```
const fetchData = async ({ queryKey }) => {
  const { someVariable } = queryKey[0];
  ...
};
```

In the preceding snippet, we destructure our `queryKey` from our `QueryFunctionContext` object. Then, since our object will be in the first position of the query key, we can destructure the value we need from our object there.

Now that you understand the two required options of every `useQuery` hook, we can start looking at what it returns.

What does useQuery return?

When using the `useQuery` hook, it returns a couple of values. To access these values, you can just assign the return of the hook to a variable or destructure the values from the return of the hook.

You can do this in the following way:

```
const values = useQuery(...);
const { data, error, status, fetchStatus }= useQuery(...);
```

In this snippet, we can see the two different ways to access the return values of the `useQuery` hook.

In this section, we'll review the following returns of the `useQuery` hook:

- `data`
- `error`
- `status`
- `fetchStatus`

data

This variable is the last successfully resolved data returned from your query function.

This is how you can use the `data` variable:

```
const App = () => {
  const { data } = useQuery({
    queryKey: ["api"],
    queryFn: fetchData,
  });

  return (
    <div>
      {data ? data.hello : null}
    </div>
  );
};
```

In this snippet, we do the following:

1. We destructure our `data` variable from our `useQuery` hook.
2. On our return, we check if we already have data from our query. When we do, we render it.

When the query executes initially, this data will be undefined. Once it finishes executing and the query function successfully resolves your data, we will have access to the data. If, for some reason, our query function promise rejects, then we can use the next variable: `error`.

error

The `error` variable lets you access the error object returned from your query function after failing.

This is how you can use the `error` variable:

```
const App = () => {
  const { error } = useQuery({
    queryKey: ["api"],
    queryFn: fetchData,
  });

  return (
    <div>
      {error ? error.message : null}
    </div>
  );
};
```

In the preceding snippet, we do the following:

1. We destructure our `error` variable from our `useQuery` hook.
2. On our return, we check if we have any errors. If we do, we render the `error` message.

When the query executes initially, the `error` value will be null. If, for some reason, the query function rejects and throws an error, then this error will be assigned to our `error` variable.

In both the `data` and `error` examples, we checked if they were defined so that we could let our application users know the current status of our query. To make this easier and help you craft a better user experience for your application, the `status` variable was added.

status

When performing a query, the query can go through several states. These states help you give more feedback to your user. For you to know what the current state of your query is, the `status` variable was created.

Here are the states that the `status` variable can have:

- `loading`: No query attempt has finished and there is still no cached data yet.
- `error`: There was an error while performing a query. Whenever this is the status, the `error` property will receive the error returned from the query function.
- `success`: Your query was successful and it has returned data. Whenever this is the status, the `data` property will receive the successful data from the query function.

This is how you can use the `status` variable:

```
const App = () => {
  const { status, error, data } = useQuery({
    queryKey: ["api"],
    queryFn: fetchData,
  });

  if(status === "loading") {
    return <div>Loading...</div>
  }

  if(status === "error") {
    return <div>There was an unexpected error:
      {error.message}</div>
  }

  return (
    <div>
        {data.hello}
    </div>
  );
};
```

In the preceding snippet, we are leveraging the `status` variable to create a better user experience for our users. This is what we are doing:

1. We start by destructuring the `status` variable from the `useQuery` hook.
2. We check if `status` is loading. This means that we still don't have any data and our query has finished. If this is the case, we render a loading indicator.
3. If our `status` is not loading, we check if there was any error during our query. If our `status` equals `error`, then we need to destructure our `error` variable and display the error message.
4. Finally, if our `status` is also not an error, then we can safely assume that our `status` equals success; therefore, we should have our `data` variable with the data our query function returned and we can display it to our user.

Now, you know how to use the `status` variable. For convenience, React Query also introduced some Boolean variants to help us identify each state. They are as follows:

- `isLoading`: Your `status` variable is in the loading state
- `isError`: Your `status` variable is in the error state
- `isSuccess`: Your `status` variable is in the success state

Let's rewrite our previous snippet leveraging our `status` Boolean variants:

```
const App = () => {
  const { isLoading, isError, error, data } = useQuery({
    queryKey: ["api"],
    queryFn: fetchData,
  });

  if(isLoading) {
    return <div>Loading...</div>
  }

  if(isError) {
    return <div>There was an unexpected error:
      {error.message}</div>
  }

  return (
    <div>
      {data.hello}
```

```
      </div>
  );
};
```

As you can see, the code is similar. All we had to do was replace our `status` variable with `isLoading` and `isError` in the destructuring and then use the `isLoading` and `isError` variables in the respective status check.

Now, the `status` variable gives you information about your query data. However, this is not the only status variable that React Query has. In the next section, you will be introduced to `fetchStatus`.

fetchStatus

With React Query v3, they found that there was an issue when handling scenarios where the user would go offline. If the user triggered a query but for some reason lost connection during the request, the `status` variable would stay pending in the loading state until the user got the connection back and the query was automatically retried.

To deal with this type of issue, in React Query v4, they introduced a new property called `networkMode`. This property can have three states, but by default, it will use the online one. The good thing is that this mode enables you to use the `fetchStatus` variable.

The `fetchStatus` variable gives you information about your query function.

Here are the states this variable can have:

- `fetching`: Your query function is currently executing. This means that it's currently fetching.
- `paused`: Your query wanted to fetch but due to a lost connection, it has now stopped executing. This means that it's currently paused.
- `idle`: The query is not doing anything at the moment. This means that it's currently idle.

Now, let's learn how to use the `fetchStatus` variable:

```
const App = () => {
  const { fetchStatus, data } = useQuery({
    queryKey: ["api"],
    queryFn: fetchData,
  });

  if(fetchStatus === "paused") {
    return <div>Waiting for your connection to return...
      </div>
```

```
  }

  if(fetchStatus === "fetching") {
    return <div>Fetching...</div>
  }

  return (
    <div>
      {data.hello}
    </div>
  );
};
```

In the preceding snippet, we are leveraging the fetchStatus variable to create a better user experience for our users. This is what we are doing:

1. We start by destructuring the fetchStatus variable from the return of our useQuery hook.
2. We then check if the current state of our fetchStatus is paused. If this is true, then right now, there is no network connection, so we let our user know.
3. If the previous If check is false, then we can validate if the current state of our fetchStatus is fetching. If the previous If check is true, then right now, the query function is running, so we let our user know.
4. If we are not fetching, then we can assume our query function's fetchStatus is idle; therefore, it has already finished fetching, so we should have the returned data.

Now, you know how to use the fetchStatus variable. Just like for the status variable, React Query also introduced some Boolean variants to help identify two of these statuses. They are as follows:

- isFetching: Your fetchStatus variable is in the fetching state
- isPaused: Your fetchStatus variable is in the paused state

Let's rewrite our previous snippet leveraging our fetchStatus Boolean variants:

```
const App = () => {
  const { isFetching, isPaused, data } = useQuery({
    queryKey" [""pi"],
    queryFn: fetchData,
  });
```

```
  if(isPaused) {
    return <div>Waiting for your connection to return...
      </div>
  }

  if(isFetching) {
    return <div>Fetching...</div>
  }

  return (
    <div>
      {data.hello}
    </div>
  );
};
```

As you can see from the snippet, the code is quite similar. All we had to do was replace our `fetchStatus` variable with `isFetching` and `isPaused` in the destructuring and then use these `isFetching` and `isPaused` variables in the respective `fetchStatus` check.

Now that we are aware of the values our `useQuery` hook returns, let's see how we can customize the same hook with the use of some options.

Commonly used options explained

When using the `useQuery` hook, more options can be passed into it than the query key and query function. These options help you craft a better developer experience, as well as a better user experience.

In this section, we'll look at some options that are more common and very important for you to be aware of.

Here are the options we'll cover:

- `staleTime`
- `cacheTime`
- `retry`
- `retryDelay`
- `enabled`

- `onSuccess`
- `onError`

staleTime

The `staleTime` option is the duration in milliseconds until query data is no longer considered *fresh*. When the set time elapses, a query is called *stale*.

While the query is *fresh*, it will be pulled from the cache without triggering a new request to update the cache. When the query is marked as *stale*, data will still be pulled from the cache but an automatic refetch of the query can be triggered.

By default, all queries use `staleTime` set to `0`. This means that all cached data will be considered *stale* by default.

This is how we can configure `staleTime`:

```
useQuery({
  staleTime: 60000,
});
```

In this snippet, we define that the query data of this hook will be considered *fresh* for one minute.

cacheTime

The `cacheTime` option is the duration in milliseconds that the data in your cache that is inactive remains in memory. Once this time passes, the data will be garbage collected.

By default, queries are marked as inactive when they have no active instance of a `useQuery` hook. When this happens, this query data will be held in the cache for 5 minutes. After these 5 minutes, this data will be garbage collected.

This is how to use the `cacheTime` option:

```
useQuery({
  cacheTime: 60000,
});
```

In the snippet, we define that after our query is inactive for 1 minute, the data will be garbage collected.

retry

The `retry` option is a value that indicates whether your query will retry or not when it fails. When `true`, it will retry until it succeeds. When `false`, it won't retry.

This property can also be a number. When it is a number, the query will retry that specified number of times.

By default, all queries that are failing will be retried three times.

This is how to use the `retry` option:

```
useQuery({
  retry: false,
});
```

In this snippet, we set the `retry` option as `false`. This means that when failing to fetch a query, this hook won't retry to fetch the data.

We can also configure the `retry` option this way:

```
useQuery({
  retry: 1,
});
```

In this snippet, we set the `retry` option with the number 1. This means that if this hook fails to fetch a query, then it will only retry the request once.

retryDelay

`retryDelay` option is the delay to apply before the next retry attempt in milliseconds.

By default, React Query uses an exponential backoff delay algorithm to define the retry timing between retries.

This is how to use the `retryDelay` option:

```
useQuery({
  retryDelay: (attempt) => attempt * 2000,
});
```

In the snippet, we define a linear backoff function as our `retryDelay` option. Every time there is a retry, this function receives the attempt number and multiplies it by 2000. This means that the time between every retry will be 2 seconds longer.

enabled

The `enabled` option is a Boolean value that indicates when your query can run or not.

By default, this value is `true`, so all queries are enabled.

This is how we can use the `enabled` option:

```
useQuery({
  enabled: arrayVariable.length > 0
});
```

In this snippet, we assign the return of the expression evaluation to the `enabled` option. This means that whenever the length of `arrayVariable` is greater than 0, this query will execute.

onSuccess

The `onSuccess` option is a function that will be triggered when your query is successful while fetching.

This is how we can use the `onSuccess` option:

```
useQuery({
  onSuccess: (data) => console.log("query was successful",
    data),
});
```

In this snippet, we pass an arrow function to our `onSuccess` option. When our query fetches successfully, this function will be called with our `data`. We then use this `data` to log to our `console`.

onError

The `onError` option is a function that will be triggered when your query fails while fetching.

This is how we can use the `onError` option:

```
useQuery({
  onError: (error) => console.log("query was unsuccessful",
    error.message),
});
```

In this snippet, we pass an arrow function to our `onError` option. When the query fails, this function will be called with the `thrown` error. We then log the error in our `console`.

As you can see, the `useQuery` hook supports a lot of options and the ones that were presented were only the tip of the iceberg. In the upcoming sections and chapters, you'll be introduced to more, so prepare yourself!

You are now familiar with the `useQuery` hook and should be able to use it to start fetching your server state data. Now, let's see some patterns and ways we can use this hook to deal with some common server state challenges.

Refetching data with useQuery

Refetching is an important part of managing our server state. Sometimes, you need your data to be updated because your data has become stale or just because you haven't interacted with your page in a while.

Manually or automatically, React Query supports and allows you to refetch your data.

In this section, we'll see how it works and what automatic and manual ways you can leverage to refetch your data.

Automatic refetching

React Query has baked in a couple of options to make your life easier and keep your server state fresh. To do this, it automatically takes care of data refetching in certain cases.

Let's look at the things that allow React Query to perform data refetching automatically.

Query keys

Query keys are used to identify your query.

When talking about query keys previously, I mentioned several times that we should include all of our query function dependencies as part of our query key. Why did I say that?

Because whenever some of those dependencies change, so will your query key, and when your query key changes, your query with be automatically refetched.

Let's look at the following example:

```
const [someVariable, setSomeVariable] = useState(0)
useQuery({
    queryKey: ["api", someVariable],
    queryFn: fetchData,
});

return <button onClick={() => setSomeVariable
  (someVariable + 1)}> Click me </button>
```

In the preceding snippet, we define a useQuery hook that has someVariable as part of its query key. This query will be fetched on the initial render like usual, but when we click on our button, the someVariable value will change. The query key will also change, which will trigger a query refetch for you to get your new data.

Refetching options

There are a couple of options I did not share in the *Commonly used options explained* section. This is because they are enabled by default, and it is often better to leave them on unless they don't suit your use case.

Here are the options related to data refetching that `useQuery` has enabled by default:

- `refetchOnWindowFocus`: Whenever you focus on your current window, this option triggers a refetch. For example, if you change tabs when you return to your application, React Query will trigger a refetch of your data.
- `refetchOnMount`: Whenever your hook mounts, this option triggers a refetch. For example, when a new component that uses your hook mounts, React Query will trigger a refetch of your data.
- `refetchOnReconnect`: Whenever you lose your internet connection, this option will trigger a refetch.

One thing that is important to note is that these options will only refetch your data by default if your data is marked as stale. This refetching of data even if its stale can be configured since all these options, excluding the Boolean value, also support receiving a string with a value of `always`. When the value of these options is `always`, it will always retrigger a refetch, even if the data is not stale.

This is how to configure them:

```
useQuery({
    refetchOnMount: "always",
    refetchOnReconnect: true,
    refetchOnWindowFocus: false
});
```

In the preceding snippet, we are doing the following:

- For the `refetchOnMount` option, we always want our hook to refetch our data whenever any component using it mounts, even if the cached data is not stale
- For `refetchOnReconnect`, we want our hook to refetch our data whenever we regain connection after being offline, but only if our data is stale
- For `refetchOnWindowFocus`, we never want our hook to refetch our data on window focus

Now, one thing that might cross your mind is if there is any way to force our hook to refetch our data every couple of seconds, even if our data is not stale. Well, even if you didn't think about it, React Query allows you to do it.

React Query adds another refetch-related option called `refetchInterval`. This option allows you to specify a frequency in milliseconds for your query to refetch data.

This is how we can use it:

```
useQuery({
    refetchInterval: 2000,
    refetchIntervalInBackground: true
});
```

In this snippet, we configure our hook to always refetch every 2 seconds. We also add another option called `refetchIntervalInBackground` with `true` as its value. This option will allow your query to keep refetching, even if your window or tab is in the background.

This wraps up automatic refetching. Now, let's see how we can trigger manual refetches in our code.

Manual refetching

There are two ways to manually trigger a query refetch. You could use `QueryClient` or get the `refetch` function from the hook.

Using QueryClient

As you may recall from the previous chapter, `QueryClient` allows you to have an interface between the developer and the query cache. This allows you to leverage `QueryClient` to force a data refetch when needed.

This is how you can trigger a data refetch using `QueryClient`:

```
const queryClient = useQueryClient();
queryClient.refetchQueries({ queryKey: ["api"] })
```

In the preceding snippet, we are doing the following:

- Using the `useQueryClient` hook to get access to our `QueryClient`.
- Using `QueryClient`, we are calling one of the functions it exposes, called `refetchQueries`. This function allows you to trigger a refetch of all the queries that match the given query key. In this snippet, we are triggering a request for all queries that have the `["api"]` query key.

Using the refetch function

Every `useQuery` hook exposes a `refetch` function for convenience. This function will allow you to trigger a refetch for just that query.

This is how you can do it:

```
const { refetch } = useQuery({
    queryKey: ["api"],
    queryFn: fetchData,
});
refetch()
```

In this snippet, we are destructuring the `refetch` function from our `useQuery` hook. Then, we can call that function whenever we want to force that query to refetch.

Now that you know how React Query enables you to manually and automatically refetch your data, let's see how we can create queries that depend on other queries.

Fetching dependent queries with useQuery

Sometimes, during our development process, we need to have values that are returned from one query that we can use in another query or have a query execution depend on a previous query. When this happens, we need to have what is called a dependent query.

React Query allows you to make a query depend on others via the `enabled` option.

This is how you can do it:

```
const App = () => {
  const { data: firstQueryData } = useQuery({
    queryKey: ["api"],
    queryFn: fetchData,
  });

  const canThisDependentQueryFetch = firstQueryData?.hello
    !== undefined;

  const { data: dependentData } = useQuery({
    queryKey: ["dependentApi", firstQueryData?.hello],
    queryFn: fetchDependentData,
    enabled: canThisDependentQueryFetch,
  });
  ...
```

In the preceding snippet, we are doing the following:

1. We are creating a query that will have `["api"]` as the query key and the `fetchData` function as the query function.
2. Next, we are creating a Boolean variable called `canThisDependentQueryFetch` that will check if our previous query has the data we need. This Boolean variable will help us decide if our next query can fetch.
3. Then, we are creating our second query with `["dependentAPI", firstQueryData?.hello]` as the query key, the `fetchDependentData` function as the query function, and our `canThisDependentQueryFetch` as our `Boolean` variable for the `enabled` option.

When the previous query finishes fetching the data, the `canThisDependentQueryFetch` Boolean will be set to `true` and enable this dependent query to run.

As you can see, you only need the `enabled` option to make a query depend on another one. Now, before wrapping up this chapter, let's put all your earned knowledge into practice.

Putting it all into practice

At this point, you should be able to start handling some use cases for data fetching using the `useQuery` hook.

In this section, we will look at a file with three components called `ComponentA`, `ComponentB`, and `ComponentC` that are doing some data fetching. We will use this file to review the concepts we have learned about and see if we fully understood how `useQuery` works.

Let's start with the beginning of the file:

```
import { useQuery, useQueryClient } from "@tanstack/react-query";

const fetchData = async ({ queryKey }) => {
  const { apiName } = queryKey[0];
  const response = await fetch(
    `https://danieljcafonso.builtwithdark.com/${apiName}`
  );
  if (!response.ok) throw new Error("Something failed in
    your request");
  return response.json();
};
```

```
const apiA = "react-query-api";
const apiB = "react-query-api-two";
```

This is what we are doing in the preceding snippet:

1. We import our `useQuery` and `useQueryClient` custom hooks from the React Query package to use in our components that will be defined in the next few snippets.
2. We create a `fetchData` function that will receive our `QueryFunctionContext`. We then destructure our `queryKey` from it. Inside this function, we do the following:

    I. We will be using an object as our query key in these examples so that we know that the first position of the array will have our query key properties, so we destructure our `apiName` from it.

    II. We use `fetch` to trigger a `GET` request to our URL and use `apiName` to help define the route.

    III. Because we are using `fetch` and not `axios`, we need to manually handle the scenario where our request failed. If our response is not OK, then we need to throw an error so that `useQuery` will be able to handle error scenarios.

    IV. If our response is valid, then we can return our response data.

3. We then create two API constant values called `apiA` and `apiB` that define the route our components will use.

Now, let's continue with our file and look at our first component, called `ComponentA`:

```
const ComponentA = () => {
  const { data, error, isLoading, isError, isFetching } =
    useQuery({
    queryKey: [{ queryIdentifier: "api", apiName: apiA }],
    queryFn: fetchData,
    retry: 1,
  });

  if (isLoading) return <div> Loading data... </div>;

  if (isError)
    return (
      <div> Something went wrong... Here is the error:
        {error.message}</div>
    );
```

```
  return (
    <div>
      <p>{isFetching ? "Fetching Component A..." :
        data.hello} </p>
      <ComponentB/>
    </div>
  );
};
```

Let's review ComponentA:

1. We start by creating our query by using the useQuery hook:

    I. This query is identified with an object as the query key. This object has api as the queryIdentifier property and apiA as the apiName property.

    II. This query has the fetchData function as the query function.

    III. By using the retry option, we also specify that if this query fails to fetch, then the hook will only retry the request one time.

    IV. We also destructure data, isLoading, isError, and isFetching from the hook.

2. If no query attempt has finished and there is still no cached data, we want to render to the user that we are loading data. We use isLoading with an If check to do this.

3. If there was an error, we want to display it. We use isError to check if there was any error. If so, we render that error.

4. If our query is not loading or has an error, then we can assume it was successful. We then render a div with the following:

    - A p tag that will check if our hook isFetching. If it is fetching, it will display Fetching Component A. If not, it will display the fetched data.
    - Our ComponentB.

Now, let's look at ComponentB:

```
const ComponentB = () => {
  const { data } = useQuery({
    queryKey: [{ queryIdentifier: "api", apiName: apiB }],
    queryFn: fetchData,
    onSuccess: (data) => console.log("Component B fetched
      data", data),
```

```
  });

  return (
    <div>
      <span>{data?.hello}</span>
      <ComponentC parentData={data} />
    </div>
  );
};
```

This is what we are doing in `ComponentB`:

1. We start by creating our query by using the `useQuery` hook:

    I. This query is identified with an object as the query key. This object has `api` as the `queryIdentifier` property and `apiB` as the `apiName` property.

    II. This query has the `fetchData` function as the query function.

    III. We use the `onSuccess` option and pass it a function that will receive our `data` and log it on our `console`, as well as an indication that this component has fetched the data.

    IV. We also destructure `data` from the hook.

2. We then return a `div` to be rendered with the following:

    - Our `hello` property from our fetched data. One thing that you might see is that we used the `?.` operator. We leverage optional chaining here to make sure there is no error, and we only render our `hello` property when our data is defined.
    - Our `ComponentC`. This component will receive our `ComponentB` data as its `parentData` prop.

Let's wrap up our file review by looking at `ComponentC`:

```
const ComponentC = ({ parentData }) => {
  const { data, isFetching } = useQuery({
    queryKey: [{ queryIdentifier: "api", apiName: apiA }],
    queryFn: fetchData,
    enabled: parentData !== undefined,
  });
  const queryClient = useQueryClient();

  return (
```

```
    <div>
      <p>{isFetching ? "Fetching Component C..." :
        data.hello} </p>
      <button
        onClick={() =>
          queryClient.refetchQueries({
            queryKey: [{ queryIdentifier: "api",
              apiName: apiA }],
          })
        }
      >
        Refetch Parent Data
      </button>
    </div>
  );
};

export default ComponentA;
```

So, this is what is happening in `ComponentC`:

1. We start by creating our query by using the `useQuery` hook:

    I. This query is identified with an object as the query key. This object has `api` as the `queryIdentifier` property and `apiA` as the `apiName` property.

    II. This query has the `fetchData` function as the query function.

    III. We use the `enabled` option to make this query depend on `parentData`; therefore, this query will only run after the query in `ComponentB` finishes and resolves data.

    IV. We destructure `data` and `isFetching` from the hook.

2. We use the `useQueryClient` hook to get access to our `QueryClient`.

3. Finally, we return a `div` that will be rendered with the following:

    - A `p` tag that will check if our hook `isFetching`. If it is fetching, it displays `Fetching Component C`. If not, it displays the fetched data.
    - A button that, when clicked, will use `queryClient` to refetch the query whose query key has `api` as the `queryIdentifier` property and `apiA` as the `apiName` property. This means that on this button click, both `useQuery` in `ComponentA` and `useQuery` in `ComponentC` will refetch some data.

Also, in the preceding snippet, we do a default export of our `ComponentA`, so it is the entry point in this file.

Now that we've seen the code file, let's review the life cycle of the hooks and understand what is happening in the background:

- When `ComponentA` renders, the following occurs:
  - An instance of `useQuery` with the `[{ queryIdentifier: "api", apiName: apiA }]` query key mounts:
    - Since this is the first mount, there is no cache nor previous requests, so our query will start fetching our data, and its `status` will be loading. Also, our query function will receive our query key as part of `QueryFunctionContext`.
    - When our data fetching succeeds, the data will be cached under the `[{ queryIdentifier: "api", apiName: apiA }]` query key.
    - Since we are assuming the default `staleTime`, which is 0, the hook will mark its data as stale.
- When `ComponentA` renders `ComponentB`, the following occurs:
  - An instance of `useQuery` with the `[{ queryIdentifier: "api", apiName: apiB }]` query key mounts:
    - Since this is the first mount, there is no cache nor previous requests, so our query will start fetching our data, and its `status` will be loading. Also, our query function will receive our query key as part of `QueryFunctionContext`.
    - When our data fetching succeeds, the data will be cached under the `[{ queryIdentifier: "api", apiName: apiB }]` query key and the hook will call the `onSuccess` function.
    - Since we are assuming the default `staleTime`, which is 0, the hook will mark its data as stale.
- When `ComponentB` renders `ComponentC`, the following occurs:
  - An instance of `useQuery` with the `[{ queryIdentifier: "api", apiName: apiA }]` query key mounts:
    - As this hook has the same query key as the hook in `ComponentA`, the hook will already have cached data under it, so the data is immediately accessible.
    - Since this query was marked as stale after the previous fetch, this hook needs to refetch it, but it needs to wait for the query to be enabled first since this query depends on us having the data of `ComponentB` first.

- Once it's been enabled, the query will trigger a refetch. This makes `isFetching` on both `ComponentA` and `ComponentC` to be `true`.
- Once the fetch request succeeds, the data will be cached under the `[{ queryIdentifier: "api", apiName: apiA }]` query key, and the query is marked as stale again.

- Now, considering it is the parent component, let's picture a scenario where `ComponentA` unmounts:
  - Since there is no longer any instance of the query with the `[{ queryIdentifier: "api", apiName: apiA }]` query key active, the default cache timeout of 5 minutes is set
  - Once 5 minutes pass, the data under this query is deleted and garbage collected
  - Since there is no longer any instance of the query with the `[{ queryIdentifier: "api", apiName: apiB }]` query key active, the default cache timeout of 5 minutes is set
  - Once 5 minutes pass, the data under this query is deleted and garbage collected

If you managed to keep track of this previous process and the life cycle of your queries during their usage, then congratulations: you understand how `useQuery` works!

Summary

In this chapter, we learned about the `useQuery` custom hook and how it allows you to fetch and cache your data by using its required options, called query key and query function. You learned how to define your query key and how your query function allows you to use any data-fetching client such as GraphQL or REST, so long it returns a promise or throws an error.

You also learned about some of the things that the `useQuery` hook returns, such as the query's `data` and `error`. For you to craft a better user experience, you were also introduced to `status` and `fetchStatus`.

For you to customize your developer experience and take it to the next level, you learned about some commonly used options you can use to customize your `useQuery` hook and make it behave as you want it to. For your convenience, here are the compiled defaults to be aware of:

- `staleTime`: 0
- `cacheTime`: 5 * 60 * 1,000 (5 minutes)
- `retry`: 3
- `retryDelay`: Exponential backoff delay algorithm
- `enabled`: True

Before wrapping up, you learned about some patterns for dealing with server state challenges such as refetching and dependent queries.

Finally, you put everything you learned into practice and reviewed an example that showed you how to leverage all this knowledge and how the `useQuery` hook works internally when you do.

In *Chapter 5, More Data-Fetching Challenges*, you will continue to learn how you can use the `useQuery` hook to solve some more common server state challenges, such as data prefetching, paginated requests, and infinite queries. You will also put the DevTools to use to help you debug your queries.

5
More Data-Fetching Challenges

By now, you must be familiar with how React Query enables you to fetch data with the help of `useQuery`. You even learned how to deal with some common challenges that the server state brings you.

In this chapter, you will learn how to deal with some more server state challenges. You will understand how you can perform parallel queries and, in the process, get to know a variant of your `useQuery` hook that makes it easier, called `useQueries`.

You will again leverage `QueryClient` to deal with data prefetching, query invalidation, and query cancelation. You will even learn how to customize the methods you use to do these things by using some filters.

Pagination and **infinite lists** are common UI patterns, and you will leverage your knowledge to build them while learning more about `useQuery` and even meeting another variant called `useInfiniteQuery`.

By the end of this chapter, you will use the Devtools once again to look inside your queries and enhance your debugging of them.

In this chapter, we'll be covering the following topics:

- Building parallel queries
- Leveraging `QueryClient`
- Creating paginated queries
- Creating infinite queries
- Debugging your queries with Devtools

Technical requirements

All the code examples for this chapter can be found on GitHub at `https://github.com/PacktPublishing/State-management-with-React-Query/tree/feat/chapter_5`.

Building parallel queries

A typical pattern that we often find the need to use is parallel queries. Parallel queries are queries that are executed at the same time to avoid having sequential network requests, often called network waterfalls.

Parallel queries help you avoid network waterfalls by firing all the requests simultaneously.

React Query allows us to perform parallel queries in two ways:

- Manually
- Dynamically

Manual parallel queries

This would probably be how you would do parallel queries if I asked you to do it right now. It involves just writing any number of `useQuery` hooks side by side.

This pattern is great when you have a fixed number of parallel queries you want to execute. This means that the number of queries you will perform will always be the same and not change.

This is how you can write parallel queries following this method:

```
const ExampleOne = () => {
  const { data: queryOneData } = useQuery({
    queryKey: [{ queryIdentifier: "api", username:
      "userOne" }],
    queryFn: fetchData,
  });
  const { data: queryTwoData } = useQuery({
    queryKey: [{ queryIdentifier: "api", username:
      "userTwo" }],
    queryFn: fetchData,
  });
  const { data: queryThreeData } = useQuery({
    queryKey: [{ queryIdentifier: "api", username:
      "userThree" }],
    queryFn: fetchData,
```

```
  });

  return (
    <div>
      <p>{queryOneData?.hello}</p>
      <p>{queryTwoData?.hello}</p>
      <p>{queryThreeData?.hello}</p>
    </div>
  );
};
```

In the preceding snippet, we create three different queries by adding different query keys to all of them. These queries will all be fetched in parallel, and once the query function is resolved, we will have access to their data. We then use this data to render their `hello` property inside p tags.

Dynamic parallel queries

While manual parallel queries fit most scenarios, if your query number varies, you won't be able to use it without breaking the rules of hooks. To deal with this issue, React Query created a custom hook called **useQueries**.

`useQueries` allows you to dynamically call as many queries as you want. Here is its syntax:

```
const queryResults = useQueries({
  queries: [
    { queryKey: ["api", "queryOne"], queryFn: fetchData },
    { queryKey: ["api", "queryTwo"], queryFn: fetchData }
  ]
})
```

As you can see from the preceding snippet, the `useQueries` hook receives an array of queries in its `queries` property. These queries can even receive options if you want, so the mental model you should have here is that these queries can be customized the same way as a `useQuery` hook.

The `useQueries` hook will return an array with all your query results.

Now that you are aware of how `useQueries` works, let's put it to practice in the following snippet:

```
const usernameList = ["userOne", "userTwo", "userThree"];

const ExampleTwo = () => {
```

```
  const multipleQueries = useQueries({
    queries: usernameList.map((username) => {
      return {
        queryKey: [{ queryIdentifier: "api", username }],
        queryFn: fetchData,
      };
    }),
  });

  return (
    <div>
      {multipleQueries.map(({ data, isFetching }) => (
        <p>{isFetching ? "Fetching data..." : data.hello}
        </p>
      ))}
    </div>
  );
};
```

In the preceding snippet, we do the following:

1. We create a `usernameList` string array to help us create some dynamic queries.
2. Inside our `useQueries` hook, for each instance inside `usernameList`, we create a respective query with its query key and query function.
3. We use the result of our `useQueries` hook; for each item inside of it, we leverage `isFetching` to display to the user that we are fetching data. If it is not fetching data, then we assume we already did our request, and we show the fetched data.

Now that you know how to leverage `useQuery` and `useQueries` to perform parallel queries, let us see how you can leverage `QueryClient` to solve some more server-state challenges.

Leveraging QueryClient

As you are aware, `QueryClient` allows you to interact with your cache.

In the previous chapter, we saw how `QueryClient` could be leveraged to trigger refetching a query. What we haven't seen yet is how `QueryClient` can be used for much more things.

To use `QueryClient` in your components, you can leverage the `useQueryClient` hook to access it. Then, all you have to do is call the method you need.

In this section, we'll see how you can use `QueryClient` to solve more server state challenges such as the following:

- Query invalidation
- Prefetching
- Query cancelation

Before we start query invalidation, one thing to be aware of is that some of these methods, namely the ones we are going to see, can receive certain query filters to help you match with the right queries.

In the previous chapter, we saw the following example for query refetching:

```
queryClient.refetchQueries({ queryKey: ["api"] })
```

The preceding snippet is an example of where we can provide a filter to the `refetchQueries` method. In this scenario, we are trying to refetch all the queries that either match or start with the query key, `["api"]`.

Now, you can use more filters other than the query key. The filters that are used in the `QueryClient` methods, typically called `QueryFilters`, support filtering by things such as the following:

- Query key
- Query type
- Whether the query is stale or fresh
- `fetchStatus`
- A predicate function

Here are some examples of using `QueryFilters`.

In the following example, we use the `type` filter with the `active` value to refetch all the queries that are currently active:

```
queryClient.refetchQueries({ type: "active" })
```

In the following example, we use the `stale` filter with `true` as a value to refetch all the queries whose `staleTime` has elapsed and are now considered stale:

```
queryClient.refetchQueries({ stale: true })
```

In the following example, we use the `fetchStatus` filter with `idle` as a value to refetch all the queries that are currently not fetching anything:

```
queryClient.refetchQueries({ fetchStatus: "idle"})
```

In the following example, we use the `predicate` property and pass an anonymous function to it. This function will receive the query being verified and access its current status; if this status is an error, then the function will return `true`. This means that all queries whose status is currently an error will refetch.

```
queryClient.refetchQueries({
        predicate: (query) => query.state.status ===
          "error",
})
```

Now, you don't need to pass only one filter. You can send a combination of filters as follows:

```
queryClient.refetchQueries({ queryKey: ["api"], stale: true
  })
```

In the preceding example, we refetch all stale queries whose query key begins with `["api"]`.

If you don't want to pass any filter and want the method to apply to all queries, you can opt not to pass any filters like this:

```
queryClient.refetchQueries()
```

This example will refetch all the queries.

You are now familiar with `QueryFilters` and can see some of the server-state challenges involved. Let's start with query invalidation.

Query invalidation

Sometimes, independent of your configured `staleTime`, your data will become stale. Why, you ask? Well, sometimes, it might be because of mutations you have performed; other times, it might be because another user somewhere interacted with your server state.

When this happens, you can leverage your `QueryClient` **invalidateQueries** method to mark your queries as stale.

Here is the `invalidateQueries` method syntax:

```
queryClient.invalidateQueries({ queryKey: ["api"] })
```

By calling `invalidateQueries`, every query that matches or starts with `["api"]` will be marked as `stale`, overriding its `staleTime` if configured. If your query is active because a `useQuery` hook rendered is using it, then React Query will take care of refetching that query.

Let us now put this into practice with the following example:

```
const QueryInvalidation = () => {
  const { data } = useQuery({
    queryKey: [{ queryIdentifier: "api", username:
      "userOne" }],
    queryFn: fetchData,
  });
  const queryClient = useQueryClient();

  return (
    <div>
      <p>{data?.hello}</p>
      <button
        onClick={() =>
          queryClient.invalidateQueries({
            queryKey: [{ queryIdentifier: "api" }],
          })
        }
      >
        Invalidate Query
      </button>
    </div>
  );
};
```

In the preceding snippet, we have an example of invalidating a query. This is what we are doing:

1. Creating a query identified by the `[{ queryIdentifier: "api", username: "userOne" }]` query key
2. Getting access to `queryClient`
3. Rendering our query data and button for which `onClick` will invalidate all queries that match or contain `[{ queryIdentifier: "api" }]` as part of its query key

When the user clicks on the **Invalidate Query** button because the created query includes `[{ queryIdentifier: "api" }]` as part of its query key, that query data will be marked immediately as `stale`. Since this query is being rendered now, it will automatically be refetched in the background.

Prefetching

You want your user experience to be the best possible one. This sometimes involves understanding what the users want even before they do. This is where prefetching can help you.

When you can predict that your user might want to do something that inevitably triggers a query, you can leverage that knowledge and prefetch your query to save some future time for your users.

`QueryClient` allows you to access a method called **prefetchQuery** to prefetch your data.

Here is the `prefetchQuery` method syntax:

```
queryClient.prefetchQuery({
    queryKey: ["api"],
    queryFn: fetchData
});
```

`prefetchQuery` requires a query key and query function. This method will try to fetch your data and cache it under the given query key. *This is an asynchronous method*; therefore, you will need to wait for it to complete.

Let us now see a practical example of when we can prefetch our data with our `ExamplePrefetching` component:

```
const ExamplePrefetching = () => {
  const [renderComponent, setRenderComponent] =
    useState(false);
  const queryClient = useQueryClient();

  const prefetchData = async () => {
    await queryClient.prefetchQuery({
      queryKey: [{ queryIdentifier: "api", username:
        "userOne" }],
      queryFn: fetchData,
      staleTime: 60000
    });
  };
```

```
  return (
    <div>
      <button onMouseEnter={prefetchData} onClick={() =>
      setRenderComponent(true)}> Render Component </button>
      {renderComponent ? <PrefetchedDataComponent /> : null
        }
    </div>
  );
};
```

In the preceding snippet, we create our `ExamplePrefetching` component. Here is what it does:

1. It creates a state variable that will be used to allow us to render `PrefetchedDataComponent`.
2. It gets access to `queryClient`.
3. It creates a function called `prefetchData` where we call the `prefetchQuery` method and cache the returned data under the `[{ queryIdentifier: "api", username: "userOne" }]` query key. We also give it a `staleTime` of 1 minute, so after calling this query, the data will be considered fresh for 1 minute.
4. Create a button that, when clicked, will change our state variable to allow us to render `PrefetchedDataComponent`. This button also has an `onMouseEnter` event that will trigger our data prefetching.

Let us now look at our `PrefetchedDataComponent` component:

```
const PrefetchedDataComponent = () => {
  const { data } = useQuery({
    queryKey: [{ queryIdentifier: "api", username:
      "userOne" }],
    queryFn: fetchData,
  });

  return <div>{data?.hello}</div>;
};
```

In the preceding snippet, we can see `PrefetchedDataComponent`. This component has a query that is identified by the `[{ queryIdentifier: "api", username: "userOne" }]` query key. When this data exists, it will be rendered inside `div`.

So, let's review the flow of these two components for a user:

1. `ExamplePrefetching` is rendered.
2. The user will see a button saying **Render Component**.
3. The user puts their mouse over the button to click on it. At this time, we predict that the user will click on the button, so we trigger the data prefetching. Once the data has been prefetched, it is cached under the `[{ queryIdentifier: "api", username: "userOne" }]` query key.
4. The user clicks on the button.
5. `PrefetchedDataComponent` is rendered.
6. The `useQuery` hook that is identified by the `[{ queryIdentifier: "api", username: "userOne" }]` query key will already have the data cached and marked as fresh for one minute, so it doesn't need to trigger data-fetching.
7. The user sees the prefetched data rendered.

Query cancelation

There will be times when your `useQuery` hook will unmount while it is doing a query. By default, once your promise has been resolved, this query data will still be received and cached. But, for some reason, you might want to cancel your queries if your hook unmounts in the middle of data-fetching requests. React Query can take care of this by automatically canceling your query if you desire. You can even cancel your queries manually if you want.

To allow you to cancel your queries, React Query uses a signal that can communicate with DOM requests and abort them. This signal is the **AbortSignal** object, which belongs to the **AbortController** Web API.

The `AbortSignal` signal is injected into our query function by `QueryFunctionContext`, and then it should be consumed by our data-fetching client.

Here is how we can leverage `AbortSignal` with `axios`:

```
const fetchData = async ({ queryKey, signal }) => {
  const { username } = queryKey[0];
  const { data } = await axios.get(
    `https://danieljcafonso.builtwithdark.com/
      react-query-api/${username}`,
    { signal }
  );
```

```
    return data;
};
```

In the preceding snippet, we receive `signal` from `QueryFunctionContext` and pass it as an option in our `axios` client while doing a `get` request.

If you use an alternative to `axios` such as `fetch` or `graphql-request` in a scenario in which you use GraphQL, you also need to pass `AbortSignal` to your client.

This is how you can do it using `fetch`:

```
const fetchDataWithFetch = async ({ queryKey, signal }) => {
  const { username } = queryKey[0];
  const response = await fetch(
    `https://danieljcafonso.builtwithdark.com/
      react-query-api/${username}`,
    { signal }
  );
  if (!response.ok) throw new Error("Something failed in
    your request");
  return response.json();
};
```

In the preceding snippet, we receive `signal` from `QueryFunctionContext` and pass it as an option to our `fetch` call.

If you are using a GraphQL client such as `graphql-request`, this is how you can do it:

```
const fetchGQL = async ({signal}) => {
  const endpoint = <Add_Endpoint_here>;
  const client = new GraphQLClient(endpoint)
  const {
    posts: { data },
  } = await client.request({document: customQuery,
    signal});
  return data;
};
```

In the preceding snippet, we also receive `signal` from `QueryFunctionContext` and pass it as an option in our client request.

Passing the signal to our clients is only the first step in allowing them to cancel queries. You need to trigger an automatic query cancelation or a manual one.

Manual cancelation

For manually canceling a query, `QueryClient` gives you access to the **cancelQueries** method.

Here is the `cancelQueries` method syntax:

```
queryClient.cancelQueries({ queryKey: ["api"] })
```

By calling `cancelQueries`, every query that matches or starts with `["api"]` that is currently fetching and that has received `AbortSignal` will be aborted.

Automatic cancelation

When a component using your hook unmounts and your query is currently fetching, if you pass `AbortSignal` to your client, React Query will abort your query by canceling the promise.

Let us see how React Query leverages `AbortSignal` to cancel your query with the next examples. First, we start by configuring our query function:

```
const fetchData = async ({ queryKey, signal }) => {
  const { username } = queryKey[0];
  const { data } = await axios.get(
    `https://danieljcafonso.builtwithdark.com/
      react-query-api/${username}`,
    { signal }
  );
  return data;
};
```

In the preceding snippet, we create a `fetchData` function that will receive `QueryContextObject`. From it, we get access to `signal` and pass it to our `axios` client.

Now, let us see our components:

```
const ExampleQueryCancelation = () => {
  const [renderComponent, setRenderComponent] =
    useState(false);

  return (
    <div>
```

```
      <button onClick={() => setRenderComponent
        (!renderComponent)}>
        Render Component
      </button>
      {renderComponent ? <QueryCancelation /> : null}
    </div>
  );
};
```

In the preceding snippet, we have a component called `ExampleQueryCancelation`. This component will render and unmount a component called `QueryCancelation` wherever a user clicks on a button.

Let's now see the `QueryCancelation` component:

```
const QueryCancelation = () => {
  const { data } = useQuery({
    queryKey: [{ queryIdentifier: "api", username:
      "userOne" }],
    queryFn: fetchData,
  });
  const queryClient = useQueryClient();

  return (
    <div>
      <p>{data?.hello}</p>
      <button
        onClick={() =>
          queryClient.cancelQueries({
            queryKey: [{ queryIdentifier: "api" }],
          })
        }
      >
        Cancel Query
      </button>
    </div>
  );
};
```

The snippet shows us the `QueryCancelation` component. In this component, we are doing the following:

1. We create a query identified by the `[{ queryIdentifier: "api", username: "userOne" }]` query key.
2. We get access to `QueryClient`.
3. We render our `data` from the query.
4. We render a button that, when clicked, will use `QueryClient` to cancel all the queries that either match or include `[{ queryIdentifier: "api" }]` in their keys.

Let us now review these components' lifetimes and how the query cancelation can work out:

1. We render the `ExampleQueryCancelation` component.
2. We click the button to render the `QueryCancelation` component.
3. `QueryCancelation` is rendered and its `useQuery` hook will trigger a request to fetch its data.
4. During this request, we click right back on the button to render `QueryCancelation`.
5. Since our request hasn't been resolved yet and our component is unmounted, React Query will abort our signal, which will cancel our request.
6. We click the button to render the `QueryCancelation` component again.
7. `QueryCancelation` is rendered, and its `useQuery` hook will trigger a request to fetch its data.
8. During this request, we click on the button to cancel our query. This will force React Query to abort our signal and cancel our request once again.

We have thus seen how `QueryClient` and some of its methods can help us solve some of our common server state challenges.

In the next section, we'll see how React Query allows us to build a common UI pattern, that is, paginated queries.

Creating paginated queries

When building an API to deal with large datasets, to avoid having your frontend deal with everything at once, you don't want to send all the available data in one request. A pattern often used to make this easier is API pagination.

If your API is paginated, you want to apply the same pattern to your application.

The good thing is that you only need to use `useQuery` and one of its options, `keepPreviousData`.

Let's look at the next examples and then understand how pagination and React Query work. First, we start with our query function:

```
const fetchData = async ({ queryKey }) => {
  const { page } = queryKey[0];
  const { data } = await axios.get(
    `https://danieljcafonso.builtwithdark.com/
      react-query-paginated?page=${page}&results=10`
  );
  return data;
};
```

In the preceding snippet, we create the function that will be used as our query function. Since this is a paginated API, we will need the page to fetch our data. As we established in the last chapter, if a variable is a dependency of our query, it needs to be added to the query key. We then destructure the page from our query key in our query function. Then, all we need to do is fetch our data and return it when the promise resolves.

Let us now see how we can build a component for displaying and fetching paginated data:

```
const PaginatedQuery = () => {
  const [page, setPage] = useState(0);

  const { isLoading, isError, error, data, isFetching,
    isPreviousData } =
    useQuery({
      queryKey: [{ queryIdentifier: "api", page }],
      queryFn: fetchData,
      keepPreviousData: true,
    });

  if (isLoading) {
    return <h2>Loading initial data...</h2>;
  }

  if (isError) {
    return <h2>{error.message}</h2>;
  }
```

```
  return (
    <>
      <div>
        {data.results.map((user) => (
          <div key={user.email}>
            {user.name.first}
            {user.name.last}
          </div>
        ))}
      </div>
      <div>
      <button
        onClick={() => setPage((oldValue) => oldValue === 0
        ? 0 : oldValue - 1)}
        disabled={page === 0}
      >
        Previous Page
      </button>
      <button
        disabled={isPreviousData}
        onClick={() => {
          if (!isPreviousData) setPage((old) => old + 1);
        }}
      >
        Next Page
      </button>
      </div>
      {isFetching ? <span> Loading...</span> : null}
    </>
  );
};
```

Let's recap in order what is happening in the preceding code block:

1. We create a state variable to hold our current selected page.
2. We create our query, which has the [{ queryIdentifier: "api", page }] query key, our fetchData function as the query function, and set keepPreviousData to

true. We set this option as `true` because, by default, whenever our query key changes, so will the query data; now, because we have a paginated API, we want to keep showing our data even if we change pages.

3. We then destructure `isLoading`, `isError`, `error`, `data`, `isFetching`, and `isPreviousData`. `isPreviousData` is used to indicate whether the data currently being shown is the previous version.
4. We then have two `if` statements to show when our query is loading, or when there is an error.
5. If we have data, we display it and two buttons to move to the next and the previous page. The button to move to the next page leverages `isPreviousData` to make sure it is disabled after we click it and move to the following query. We also display a fetching indicator.

Now that we have seen how the code is structured, let's see how it behaves when interacted with:

1. Our component is rendered, and the first page starts to be fetched.

   The `isLoading` property is set as `true`, so we render `Loading initial data`.
2. The data for the first page is resolved, so we display it.
3. We click on the **Next Page** button:

   I. The `page` value is incremented.

   II. The query key changes, so the following query starts fetching.

   III. Since we have `keepPreviousData` as `true`, we will still display the old data.

   IV. Since we are displaying old data, `isPreviousData` is set to `true`, and the **Next Page** button is disabled.

   V. The fetching indicator shows `Loading`.
4. We get the new data and display it.
5. We click on the **Previous Page** button:

   I. The page value is decremented.

   II. The query key goes back to the previous one.

   III. Since the data exists cached under this query key, it is returned.

   IV. As the data is stale, a new fetching request is triggered.

   V. The fetching indicator displays `Loading`.
6. The new data is received and displayed.

As you can see, all you need is a new option and the same old `useQuery` hook to enable you to build an application using pagination.

For the next section, let's see now how we can build infinite queries.

Creating infinite queries

Another very common UI pattern is building an infinite scroll component. In this pattern, we are presented with a list that allows us to load more data as we scroll down.

To deal with these types of lists, React Query has an alternative to the `useQuery` hook, which is another custom hook called **useInfiniteQuery**.

Using the `useInfiniteQuery` hook has many similarities to the `useQuery` one, but some things differ that we need to be aware of:

- Your data is now an object that contains the following:
  - The fetched pages
  - The `page` parameters that were used to fetch the pages
- A function called `fetchNextPage` to fetch the next page
- A function called `fetchPreviousPage` to fetch the previous page
- A Boolean state called `isFetchingNextPage` to indicate that the next page is being fetched
- A Boolean state called `isFetchingPreviousPage` to indicate that the next page is being fetched
- A Boolean state called `hasNextPage` to indicate whether the list has a next page
- A Boolean state called `hasPreviousPage` to indicate whether the list has a previous page

These last two Boolean values depend on two options that can be passed to the hook. Respectively, they are `getNextPageParam` and `getPreviousPageParam`. The functions will be responsible for picking the last or first page in the cache and checking whether its data indicates the next or previous page to be fetched. If these values exist, then the respective Boolean values will be `true`. If they return undefined, then the Boolean values will be `false`.

To use the `useInfiniteQuery` hook, you need to import it this way:

```
import { useInfiniteQuery } from "@tanstack/react-query"
```

Let us now see an example of how to use the `useInfiniteQuery` hook to build an infinite list:

```
const fetchData = async ({ pageParam = 1 }) => {
    const { data } = await axios.get(
        `https://danieljcafonso.builtwithdark.com/
        react-query-infinite?page=${pageParam}&results=10`
```

```
    );
    return data;
};
```

In the preceding snippet, we set up the function to be used as the infinite query function. The hook will pass `pageParam` in `QueryFunctionContext` so that we can leverage it to fetch our data. Like the query function in the `useQuery` hook, this query function needs to either resolve the data or throw an error, so all the same principles learned previously apply.

The next snippet will show us our `InfiniteScroll` component:

```
const InfiniteScroll = () => {
  const {
    isLoading,
    isError,
    error,
    data,
    fetchNextPage,
    isFetchingNextPage,
    hasNextPage,
  } = useInfiniteQuery({
    queryKey: ["api"],
    queryFn: fetchData,
    getNextPageParam: (lastPage, pages) => {
      return lastPage.info.nextPage;
    },
  });

  if (isLoading) {
    return <h2>Loading initial data...</h2>;
  }

  if (isError) {
    return <h2>{error.message}</h2>;
  }

  return (
    <>
```

```
        <div>
          {data.pages.map((page) =>
            page.results.map((user) => (
              <div key={user.email}>
                {user.name.first}
                {user.name.last}
              </div>
            ))
          )}
        </div>
        <button
          disabled={!hasNextPage || isFetchingNextPage}
          onClick={fetchNextPage}
        >
          {isFetchingNextPage
            ? «Loading...»
            : hasNextPage
            ? «Load More»
            : «You have no more data»}
        </button>
      </>
    );
};
```

In the preceding snippet, we have a component that renders an infinite list. This is what we are doing in the component:

1. We create `useInfiniteQuery`, which has `["api"]` as the query key and `fetchData` as the query function. It also receives an anonymous function in the `getNextPageParam` option to check whether there is still more data to be loaded on the next page.
2. We also destructure from the hook some variables needed to build our application.
3. We then have two `if` statements to show when our query is loading, or when there is an error.
4. When we have data, we map the content inside its `page` properties to render our list.

5. We also render a button that will be disabled if we don't have the next page or when we are currently fetching the next page. When clicked, this button will fetch more data. This button message will also depend on some constraints:

   - If we are fetching, the next page will show a `Loading` message
   - If we have the next page, it will show `Load more` so the user can click it to start fetching
   - If there is no more data to fetch, it will show a message letting the user know there is no more data

As we just reviewed how the component is built, let us see how it will work when interacting with it:

1. Our component renders, and the first page of the list is automatically fetched:

   - The `isLoading` property is set to `true`, so we render `Loading initial data`

2. The data for the first page of the list is resolved, so we display it.
3. At the same time, the `getNextPageParam` function checks whether we have more data on the list.
4. If there is no more data, the `hasNextPage` property is set to `false` and the button for fetching more data is disabled and displays **You have no more data**.
5. If there is more data, the `hasNextPage` property is set to `true`, and the user can click the button to fetch more data.
6. If the user clicks the button, we see the following:

   I. The next page starts fetching.
   II. The `isFetchingNextPage` value becomes `true`.
   III. The button is disabled and displays the loading message.
   IV. The data is resolved, and our data `pages` property length increases as it has the data for the new page. *Steps 3, 4,* and *5* are repeated.

With this, we just saw how the `useQuery` variant called `useInfiniteQuery` allows us to build an infinite list straightforwardly.

Before we wrap up this chapter, let's finally see how we can use the React Query Devtools to help us debug our code and see how our queries behave.

Debugging your queries with Devtools

In *Chapter 3*, you learned about React Query Devtools. At that point, you didn't know how to use queries yet, so we could not see it working. Well, now we can.

For the images you are going to see next, we are going to leverage the code we wrote when showing you the `useQueries` hook example in the *Dynamic parallel queries* section.

So that you remember, here is the code:

```
const usernameList = ["userOne", "userTwo", "userThree"];

const ExampleTwo = () => {
  const multipleQueries = useQueries({
    queries: usernameList.map((username) => {
      return {
        queryKey: [{ queryIdentifier: "api", username }],
        queryFn: fetchData,
      };
    }),
  });

  return (
    <div>
      {multipleQueries.map(({ data, isFetching }) => (
        <p>{isFetching ? "Fetching data..." : data.hello}
        </p>
      ))}
    </div>
  );
};
```

When using that code and checking our page, this is what the Devtools will present us with:

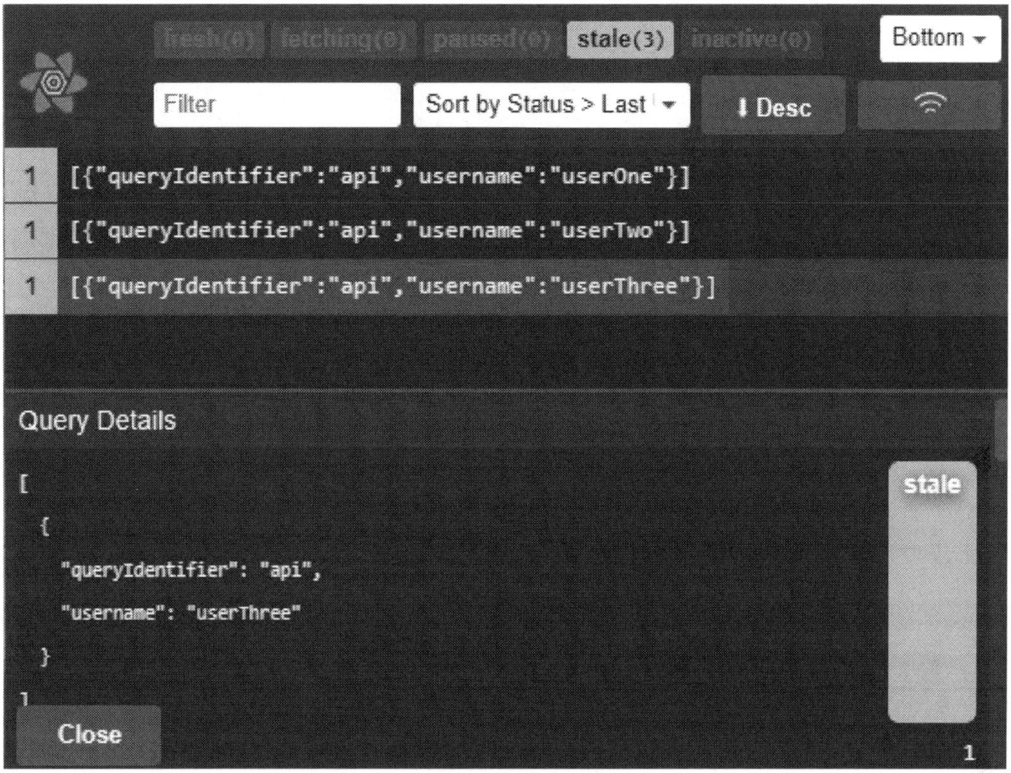

Figure 5.1 – React Query Devtools after parallel queries are executed

In the preceding figure, we can see the following things:

- We have three queries
- Each one of the queries is identified by the respective query key
- All of the queries are currently stale
- We have selected the query identified with the `[{ queryIdentifier: "api", username: "userThree" }]` query key

When we select a query, we can see the query details in our **Query Details** tab.

In the preceding figure, we can see that this query is identified by its query key and its status.

Scrolling down on the **Query Details** tab, we are also able to see the following:

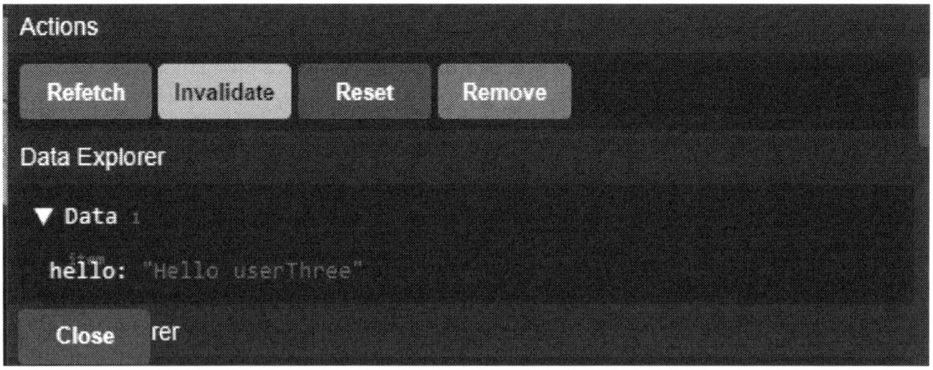

Figure 5.2 – React Query Devtools Query Details tab displaying Actions and Data Explorer

In the preceding figure, we can see that we can perform several actions for the selected query, such as refetching, invalidating, resetting, and removing it.

We are also able to see the current data of this query.

Scrolling even further down our **Query Details** tab, we can also check **Query Explorer**:

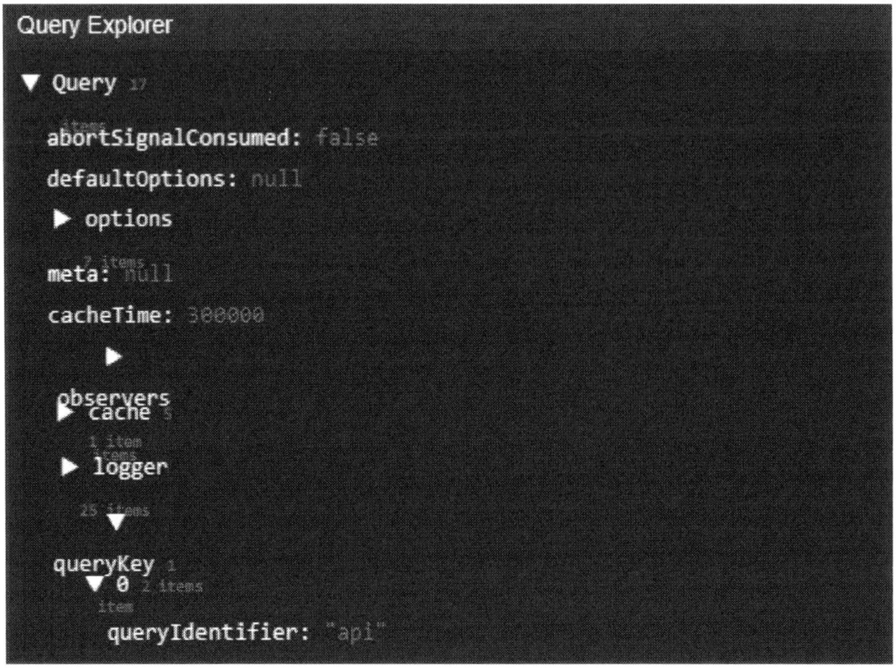

Figure 5.3 – React Query Devtools Query Details tab displaying Query Explorer

In the preceding figure, we can see **Query Explorer** for our selected query. Here, we can see the options that our query is using right now. Here, one of the things we can highlight is that this query has the default `cacheTime` of `300000`.

You are now aware of what you can see in the Devtools for each selected query.

Before wrapping up this section, let's just see what happens when we click on one of the buttons available in the **Query Details** actions:

Figure 5.4 – React Query Devtools currently fetching a query

In the preceding figure, we clicked on the **Invalidate** button for our query identified by the `[{ queryIdentifier: "api", username: "userTwo" }]` query key.

As you remember from learning about query invalidation, when we invalidate a query, it is automatically marked as `stale`, and if the query is currently being rendered, it will automatically be refetched. As you can see from the figure, this is what happened. Our query was already stale, so there was no need to mark it as `stale` again, but as it was currently being rendered on our page, React Query took care of refetching it, and we can see that in the figure.

As you saw from this section, the Devtools can save you a lot of time debugging your queries. By looking inside your queries, you can check what their data looks like if you have configured the right options, and even trigger some actions if you so desire.

Summary

In this chapter, we learned more about using the `useQuery` hook to solve some common challenges we are presented with when dealing with the server state. By now, you can handle all your data fetching needs and do it easily.

You learned about parallel queries and learned you could manually build these queries with `useQuery`. You were also introduced to one alternative of the `useQuery` hook: `useQueries`. With it, you learned how to build dynamic parallel queries.

You got to learn more about some methods of `QueryClient` that allow you to prefetch, cancel, and invalidate queries and also understood how you can leverage `QueryFilters` to customize the query matching used in these methods.

Pagination is a typical UI pattern, and now you know that you can easily build a paginated component with the help of `useQuery` and one of its options.

Another typical UI pattern is infinite scrolling. With the help of another `useQuery` variant called `useInfiniteQuery`, you learned how React Query enables you to build an application with an infinite list.

Finally, you looked inside your queries with the React Query Devtools and understood how it allows you to debug them and improve your development process.

In *Chapter 6*, *Performing Data Mutations with React Query*, we'll leave data fetching behind and move on to mutations. You'll understand how React Query enables you to perform mutations with the help of one of its custom hooks called `useMutation`. You will also leverage this hook to deal with more common server-state challenges you find in your applications and start building a better user experience in your apps by using optimistic updates.

6
Performing Data Mutations with React Query

When building applications, you won't always need to fetch data. Sometimes, you will want to create, update, or delete it. When doing these actions, your server state will have to change.

React Query allows you to change your server state by using mutations. To perform mutations, you can leverage another of React Query's custom hooks, called `useMutation`.

In this chapter, you will be introduced to the `useMutation` hook and understand how React Query allows you to create, update, and delete your server state. Similar to *Chapter 4*, during this process, you will learn about all the defaults used in your mutations. You will also be introduced to some options you can use to improve your `useMutation` experience.

Once you are familiar with `useMutation`, you will get to know how you can leverage some of its options to perform some side-effect patterns, such as manually updating your data or forcing a query to update after performing a mutation.

At the end of this chapter, we will put together all we have learned so far and apply it to do something that might improve your user experience considerably: optimistic updates.

In this chapter, we'll be covering the following topics:

- What is `useMutation` and how does it work?
- Performing side-effect patterns after mutations
- Performing optimistic updates

Technical requirements

All the code examples for this chapter can be found on GitHub at `https://github.com/PacktPublishing/State-management-with-React-Query/tree/feat/chapter_6`.

What is useMutation and how does it work?

You must be aware by now that mutations allow you to perform updates to your server state. These updates can be things such as creating data, removing data, or editing your data.

To allow you to perform mutations on your server data, React Query created a hook called `useMutation`.

Now, unlike `useQuery`, which under the default circumstances runs your query automatically as soon as the component using it renders or some dependencies of it change, `useMutation` will only run your mutation when you call one of the functions it returns from the hook instantiation called `mutate`.

To use the `useMutation` hook, you have to import it like this:

```
import { useMutation } from '@tanstack/react-query';
```

Once it is imported, you can use it to define your mutation. Here is the `useMutation` syntax:

```
const mutation = useMutation({
    mutationFn: <InsertMutationFunction>
})
```

As you can see from the preceding snippet, the `useMutation` hook only needs one required parameter for it to work, the mutation function.

What is the mutation function?

The mutation function is a function that returns a promise responsible for performing an asynchronous task. In this scenario, this asynchronous task will be our mutation.

The same principle we previously saw with the query function also applies to the mutation function. This means that, as we saw with query functions, since this function only needs to return a promise, it allows us again to use any asynchronous client of our choice. This means that REST and GraphQL are still supported, so you can use both options simultaneously if you desire.

Let us now look at an example of a mutation function using GraphQL and another using REST. These mutation functions will be leveraged to create a new user on our server state:

Mutation with GraphQL

```
import { useMutation } from "@tanstack/react-query";
import { gql, GraphQLClient } from "graphql-request";

const customMutation = gql`
mutation AddUser($user: String!, $age: Int!) {
  insert_user(object: { user: $user, age: $age }) {
    user
    age
  }
}
`;


const createUserGQL = async (user) => {
  const endpoint = <add_endpoint_here>;
  const client = new GraphQLClient(endpoint)
  return client.request(customMutation, user);
  return data;
};
 ...
const mutation = useMutation({
    mutationFn: createUserGQL
  });
```

The preceding snippet shows an example of using React Query to create a mutation with GraphQL. Here is what we are doing:

1. We start by creating our GraphQL mutation and assigning it to our `customQuery` variable.

2. We then create the `createUserGQL` function, which will be our mutation function. This function will also receive as a parameter the `user` data to be used by our mutation to create the data on the server.

3. In our `useMutation` hook, we pass our `createUserGQL` function as the mutation function to the hook.

Let us now see how to do this using REST:

Mutation with REST

```
import axios from "axios";
import {useMutation} from "@tanstack/react-query";

const createUser = async (user) => {
  return axios.post
    (`https://danieljcafonso.builtwithdark.com/name-api`,
      user);
};
  ...
const mutation = useMutation({
    mutationFn: createUser
  });
```

In the preceding snippet, we can see an example of using React Query to create a mutation with REST. Here is what we are doing:

1. We start by creating the `createUser` function, which will be our mutation function. This function will receive as a parameter the `user` data used by our mutation to create the data on the server. Here, we know we are going to be creating data on the server due to the use of the `POST` method.

2. In our `useMutation` hook, we pass to the hook our `createUser` function as the mutation function.

In the preceding example, we used `axios`, but if you prefer using `fetch` over `axios`, all you have to do is inside the `createUser` function, replace `axios` with `fetch` and apply the required changes for `fetch` to work. Here is an example of what you would need to do to use `fetch`:

```
const createUserFetch = async (user) => {
  return fetch
    (`https://danieljcafonso.builtwithdark.com/name-api`, {
    method: "POST",
    body: JSON.stringify(user),
    headers: {
      "Content-type": "application/json; charset=UTF-8",
    },
```

```
    });
};
const mutation = useMutation({
    mutationFn: createUserFetch
});
```

In the preceding snippet, we can see an example of our `createUser` function shown previously, but this time, we used `fetch` instead of `axios`.

Now that we are familiar with the mutation function, we need to understand how the `useMutation` hook leverages this function to allow us to perform our mutations. In the next section, we will learn about how the `mutate` function enables us to do this, as well as other things `useMutation` returns.

What does useMutation return?

Like `useQuery`, when using the `useMutation` hook, it returns a couple of values.

As mentioned throughout this chapter so far, to perform mutations, we need to leverage `mutate`. Now, `mutate` is not the only way to perform mutations and is also not the only thing `useMutation` returns.

In this section, we'll review the following returns of the `useMutation` hook:

- `mutate`
- `mutateAsync`
- `data`
- `error`
- `reset`
- `status`
- `isPaused`

mutate

After creating your mutation with your `useMutation` hook, you need a way to trigger it. `mutate` is the function you will need almost every time to do so.

Here is how you can use `mutate`:

```
const { mutate } = useMutation({
    mutationFn: createUser
});
mutate({ name: "username", age: 25 })
```

In this snippet, we do the following:

1. We destructure our mutate function from our useMutation hook.
2. We call the mutate function with the variables our mutation function is expecting to receive to perform our mutation.

That's it; that is how you can perform mutations with React Query. You create your mutation function, pass it to your useMutation hook, destructure mutate from it, and call it with the required parameters to perform your mutation whenever you want.

Now, the preceding snippet serves to show how you can trigger mutations by using mutate but isn't a very practical example. To help you create a mental model of how you can use mutate to perform mutations, you can refer to the following snippet:

```
import axios from "axios";
import { useMutation } from "@tanstack/react-query";
import { useState } from "react";

const createUser = async (user) => {
  return axios.post
    (`https://danieljcafonso.builtwithdark.com/name-api`,
      user);
};

const SimpleMutation = () => {
  const [name, setName] = useState("");

  const { mutate } = useMutation({
    mutationFn: createUser,
  });

  const submitForm = (e) => {
    e.preventDefault()
    mutate({ name })
  }

  return (
    <div>
```

```
      <form>
        <input
          name="name"
          type={"text"}
          onChange={(e) => setName(e.target.value)}
          value={name}
        />
        <button onClick={submitForm}>Add</button>
      </form>
    </div>
  );
};
```

In the preceding snippet, we can see an example of a simple form using a controlled component. This is what is happening in the preceding snippet:

1. We create the `createUser` mutation function, which will receive a `user` object with some data.

   Inside this function, we return the invocation of the `axios` client's `post` method, which will return the promise that `useMutation` expects to receive for its mutation function.

2. Inside our `SimpleMutation` component, we do the following:

   I.   We create a state variable to control the state of our input.

   II. We create our mutation using the `createUser` function as the mutation function and destructure `mutate` from it.

   III. We create a `submitForm` function. This function will receive the event from the form and prevent it from propagating so your page is not refreshed. After handling the event, it triggers the mutation and passes it the `name` state variable as part of the `user` object by calling `mutate`.

3. Inside our form, we create our input to handle our `name` and have React control its state.

4. We create a button with an `onClick` event to fire our `submitForm` function.

As you should understand from the preceding explanation and code, whenever we click on the **Add** button, we will trigger a `POST` request to our URL with the current value of our input.

One thing you'll also see while proceeding with this chapter is that `mutate` can also receive some options to perform side effects if you desire to. But let's leave these details for later.

While `mutate` is the staple for performing mutations in React Query, there is also another function you can use if you so desire: `mutateAsync`.

mutateAsync

While in most scenarios you will use `mutate`, sometimes you might want to access the promise that contains the result of your mutation. In these scenarios, you can use `mutateAsync`.

One thing to keep in mind while using `mutateAsync` is that you need to handle the promise yourself. This means that in an error scenario, you need to catch the error.

Here is how you can use the `mutateAsync` function:

```
const { mutateAsync } = useMutation({
  mutationFn: createUser,
});
try {
  const user = await mutateAsync({ name: "username", age:
    25 });
} catch (error) {
  console.error(error);
}
```

In the preceding snippet, we destructure the `mutateAsync` function from the `useMutation` hook:

- We need to handle potential error scenarios, so we wrap our `mutateAsync` call with a `try-catch` statement. Since this is an asynchronous function, we must wait for the data to be returned.
- If there is an error, we catch it and show an error in our console.

The preceding snippet shows how you can trigger mutations by using `mutateAsync`; as we showed in `mutate`, it doesn't seem to be a very practical example. To help you create a mental model of how you can use `mutateAsync` to perform mutations, you can see the following snippet:

```
const ConcurrentMutations = () => {
  const [name, setName] = useState("");

  const { mutateAsync: mutateAsyncOne } = useMutation({
    mutationFn: createUser,
  });
  const { mutateAsync: mutateAsyncTwo } = useMutation({
    mutationFn: registerUser,
  });
```

```
const submitForm = async (e) => {
  e.preventDefault()
  const mutationOne = mutateAsyncOne({ name })
  const mutationTwo = mutateAsyncTwo({ name })

   try {
    const data = await Promise.all([mutationOne,
      mutationTwo]);
    // do something with data
  } catch (error) {
    console.error(error);
  }
}

return (
  <div>
    <form>
      <input
        name="name"
        type={"text"}
        onChange={(e) => setName(e.target.value)}
        value={name}
      />
      <button onClick={submitForm}>Add</button>
    </form>
  </div>
);
};
```

In the preceding snippet, we can see an example of a simple form using a controlled component where we leverage `mutateAsync` to perform concurrent mutations. This is what is happening in the code:

1. We create a state variable to control the state of our input.
2. We create our first mutation using the `createUser` function as the mutation function and destructure `mutateAsync` as `mutateAsyncOne` from it.
3. We create our second mutation using the `registerUser` function as the mutation function and destructure `mutateAsync` as `mutateAsyncTwo` from it.

4. We create a `submitForm` function:
   I. This function will receive the event from the form and prevent it from propagating so your page is not refreshed.
   II. We assign the promise returned from the call of `mutationAsyncOne` with name as a parameter to our `mutationOne` variable.
   III. We assign the promise returned from the call of `mutationAsyncTwo` with name as a parameter to our `mutationTwo` variable.
   IV. We leverage the `Promise.all` method and pass it to our `mutationOne` and `mutationTwo` promises so they can be performed concurrently.
5. Inside our form, we create our input to handle our name and have React control its state.
6. We create a button with an `onClick` event to fire our `submitForm` function.

Now that you are familiar with how you can perform mutations, let's review a variable that is impacted by the success of a mutation, `data`.

data

This variable is the last successfully resolved `data` of the mutation returned from your mutation function.

Here is how you can use the `data` variable:

```
const SimpleMutation = () => {
  const { mutate, data } = useMutation({
    mutationFn: createUser,
  });

  return (
    <div>
        {data && <p>{data.data.user}</p>}
      ...

    </div>
  );
}
```

In this snippet, we do the following:

1. We destructure our `data` variable from our `useMutation` hook.
2. On our component return, we check whether we already have `data` from our mutation. If we do, we render it.

When the hook renders initially, this `data` will be undefined. Once the mutation triggers and finishes executing, and the promise returned from the mutation function successfully resolves our data, we will have access to the `data`. If for some reason our mutation function promise rejects, we can use the next variable, the `error` one.

error

The `error` variable lets you access the `error` object returned from your mutation function after failing.

Here is how you can use the `error` variable:

```
const SimpleMutation = () => {
  const { mutate, error } = useMutation({
    mutationFn: createUser,
  });

  return (
    <div>
        {error && <p>{error.message}</p>}
    ...
    </div>
  );
};
```

In the preceding snippet, we do the following:

1. We destructure our `error` variable from our `useQuery` hook.
2. On our component return, we check whether we have any errors. If we do, we render the error message.

When the hook renders initially, the `error` value will be null. If, after a mutation, for some reason the mutation function rejects and throws an error, then this error will be assigned to our `error` variable. It is important to mention here that this only applies if you are using `mutate`. If you use `mutateAsync`, you must catch the error and handle it yourself.

When using the `error` variable, there will be times for the sake of user experience when you want to clear your errors. In those scenarios, the `reset` function will be your best friend.

reset

The `reset` function allows you to reset `error` and `data` to their initial state.

This function is useful if you need to clear the current value of data or errors after running a mutation.

Here is how you can use the `reset` function:

```
const SimpleMutation = () => {
  const { mutate, data, error, reset } = useMutation({
    mutationFn: createUser,
  });

  return (
    <div>
        {error && <p>{error.message}</p>}
        {data && <p>{data.data.user}</p>}
        <button onClick={() => reset()}>Clear errors and
          data</button>
        ...
    </div>
  );
};
```

In this snippet, we do the following:

1. We destructure our `data` and `error` variables and the `reset` function from our `useMutation` hook.
2. On our component return, we check whether we already have data or errors from our mutation. When and if we do, we render them.
3. We also render a button with an `onClick` event. When clicked, this button will trigger our `reset` function to clear our `data` and `error` values.

Now, to use the `error` and `data` variables, we just check in the code whether they are defined to allow us to render them. To make this easier and once again help you craft a better user experience in your application, you can resort to using the `status` variable.

status

Like queries, when performing a mutation, the mutation can go through several states. These states help you to give more feedback to your users. For you to know what the current state of your mutation is, the `status` variable was created.

Here are the states that the `status` variable can have:

- `idle`: This is the initial status of your mutation before being executed.
- `loading`: This indicates if your mutation is currently executing.
- `error`: This indicates that there was an error while performing the last mutation. Whenever this is the status, the `error` property will receive the error returned from the mutation function.
- `success`: Your last mutation was successful, and it has returned data. Whenever this is the status, the `data` property will receive the successful data from the mutation function.

Here is how you can use the `status` variable:

```
const SimpleMutation = () => {
  const [name, setName] = useState("");

  const { mutate, status, error, data } = useMutation({
    mutationFn: createUser,
  });

  const submitForm = (e) => {
    e.preventDefault()
    mutate({ name })
  }

  return (
    <div>
      {status === "idle" && <p> Mutation hasn't run </p>}
      {status === "error" && <p> There was an error:
        {error.message} </p>}
      {status === "success" && <p> Mutation was successful:
        {data.name} </p>}
      <form>
        <input
          name="name"
```

```
            type={"text"}
            onChange={(e) => setName(e.target.value)}
            value={name}
          />
          <button disabled={status === "loading"}
            onClick={submitForm}>Add</button>
        </form>
      </div>
    );
};
```

In the preceding snippet, we are leveraging the `status` variable to create a better user experience for our users. Here is what we are doing:

1. We create a state variable to handle our controlled form.
2. We create our mutation and destructure `status` from the `useMutation` hook.
3. We create a `submitForm` function to handle our mutation submission.
4. We leverage our `status` variables to do the following in our component return:

    I. If `status` is `idle`, we render a message letting the user know our mutation hasn't run.

    II. If `status` equals `error`, we must destructure our `error` variable and display the error message.

    III. If `status` equals `success`, we must destructure our `data` variable and display it to our user.

    IV. If `status` equals `loading`, it means we are executing a mutation, so we use this to make sure we disable our **Add** button and avoid the user clicking it again while the mutation runs.

Now, you know how to use the `status` variable. For convenience, React Query also introduced some Boolean variants to help identify each state. They are as follows:

- `isIdle`: Your `status` variable is in the idle state
- `isLoading`: Your `status` variable is in the loading state
- `isError`: Your `status` variable is in the error state
- `isSuccess`: Your `status` variable is in the success state

Let's now rewrite our previous snippet leveraging our `status` Boolean variants:

```
const SimpleMutation = () => {
  const [name, setName] = useState("");
```

```
  const { mutate, isIdle, isError, isSuccess, isLoading,
    error, data } = useMutation({
    mutationFn: createUser,
  });

  const submitForm = (e) => {
    e.preventDefault()
    mutate({ name })
  }

  return (
    <div>
      {isIdle && <p> Mutation hasn't run </p>}
      {isError && <p> There was an error: {error.message}
        </p>}
      {isSuccess && <p> Mutation was successful:
        {data.name} </p>}
      <form>
        <input
          name="name"
          type={"text"}
          onChange={(e => setName(e.target.value)}
          value={name}
        />
        <button disabled={isLoading} onClick={submitForm}>
          Add</button>
      </form>
    </div>
  );
};
```

As you can see, the code is similar. All we had to do was replace our `status` variable with `isLoading`, `isError`, `isSuccess`, and `isIdle` in the destructuring part and then use these variables in the respective status check.

Unlike queries, mutations don't have a `fetchStatus` variable. Now, this doesn't mean that your mutation cannot suffer from a sudden loss of internet connection. To give more feedback to your users, the `isPaused` variable was created.

isPaused

As you should remember from *Chapter 4*, React Query introduced a new property called `networkMode`. When used in online mode, you can access a new variable in your `useMutation` hook called `isPaused`.

This Boolean variable identifies whether your mutation is currently paused due to a lost connection.

Let us see how to use the `isPaused` variable:

```
const SimpleMutation = () => {
  const [name, setName] = useState("");

  const { mutate, isPaused } = useMutation({
    mutationFn: createUser,
  });

  const submitForm = e => {
    e.preventDefault()
    mutate({ name })
  }

  return (
    <div>
      {isPaused && <p> Waiting for network to come back </p>}
      <form>
        <input
          na"e="n"me"
          typ"={"t"xt"}
          onChang€(e) => setName(e.target.value)}
          value={name}
        />
        <button disabled={isPaused} onClick={submitForm}>
          Add</button>
      </form>
    </div>
  );
};
```

In the preceding snippet, we leverage the `isPaused` variable to craft a better user experience in our application:

1. We destructure our `isPaused` variable from our `useMutation` hook.
2. In our component return, we check whether `isPaused` is `true`. If so, we render a message to let our users know. We also assign it to disable our **Add** button to avoid the user accidentally triggering another mutation.

Now that we know some of the values our `useMutation` hook returns, let's see how we can customize this hook with some options.

Commonly used mutation options explained

Like the `useQuery` hook, more options can be passed into our `useMutation` hook than just its mutation function. These options will also help us craft a better developer and user experience.

In this section, we'll see some options that are more common and very important for you to be aware of.

Here are the options we'll look at:

- `cacheTime`
- `mutationKey`
- `retry`
- `retryDelay`
- `onMutate`
- `onSuccess`
- `onError`
- `onSettled`

cacheTime

The `cacheTime` option is the duration in milliseconds that the data in your cache that is inactive remains in memory. Once this time passes, the data will be garbage collected. Note that this does not work the same way as it does with queries. If you perform a mutation, the returned data is cached, but if you perform the same mutation again while this mutation is pending, `useMutation` won't return the previous mutation data. In mutations, this option is mostly useful for preventing previous mutation data from being held in `MutationCache` indefinitely.

Here is how to use the `cacheTime` option:

```
useMutation({
  cacheTime: 60000,
});
```

In this snippet, we define that after our mutation is inactive for one minute, the data will be garbage collected.

mutationKey

Sometimes you will want to set some defaults for all your mutations by leveraging your `queryClient setMutationDefaults`.

The `mutationKey` option allows React Query to know whether it needs to apply previously configured defaults to this mutation.

Here is how to use the `mutationKey` option:

```
useMutation({
  mutationKey: ["myUserMutation"],
});
```

In the preceding snippet, we create a mutation with `["myUserMutation"]` as the mutation key. If any defaults were configured to be applied to any mutation with `["myUserMutation"]` as the mutation key, they would now be applied.

retry

The `retry` option is a value that indicates whether your mutation will retry or not when it fails. When `true`, it will retry until it succeeds. When `false`, it won't retry.

This property can also be a number. When it is a number, the mutation will retry that specified number of times.

By default, React Query will not retry a mutation on error.

Here is how to use the `retry` option:

```
useMutation({
  retry: 2,
});
```

In the snippet, we set the `retry` option to 2. This means that when failing to perform a mutation, this hook will retry performing the mutation two times.

retryDelay

The `retryDelay` option is the delay to apply before the next retry attempt in milliseconds.

By default, React Query uses an exponential backoff delay algorithm to define the retry timing between retries.

Here is how to use the `retryDelay` option:

```
useMutation({
  retryDelay: (attempt) => attempt * 2000,
});
```

In the snippet, we define a linear backoff function as our `retryDelay` option. Every time there is a retry, this function receives the attempt number and multiplies it by 2,000. This means that the time between every retry will be two seconds longer.

onMutate

The `onMutate` option is a function that will be triggered before your mutation function is fired. This function also receives the variables your mutation function will receive.

You can return values from this function that will be passed to your `onError` and `onSettled` callback functions:

```
useMutation({
  onMutate: (variables) => showNotification("Updating the
    following data:", variables),
});
```

In this snippet, we pass an arrow function to our `onMutate` option. When our mutation is triggered, this function assigned to the `onMutate` option will be called with the variables your mutation function will receive. We then use these variables to show a notification to the user about the pending mutation.

onSuccess

The `onSuccess` option is a function that will be triggered when your mutation is successful.

If a promise is returned from this function, it will be awaited and resolved. This means your mutation status will be in a loading state until the promise resolves.

This is how to use the `onSuccess` option:

```
useMutation({
  onSuccess: (data) => console.log("mutation was
    successful", data),
});
```

In the snippet, we pass an arrow function to our `onSuccess` option. When our mutation performs successfully, this function assigned to the `onSuccess` option will be called with our data. We then use this data to log a message to our console.

onError

The `onError` option is a function that will be triggered when your mutation fails.

If a promise is returned from this function, it will be awaited and resolved. This means your mutation status will be in a loading state until the promise resolves.

This is how to use the `onError` option:

```
useMutation({
  onError: (error) => console.log("mutation was
    unsuccessful", error.message),
});
```

In the snippet, we pass an arrow function to our `onError` option. When the mutation fails, this function assigned to the `onError` option will be called with the thrown error. We then log the error in our console.

onSettled

The `onSettled` option is a function that will be triggered when your mutation is either successful or fails.

If a promise is returned from this function, it will be awaited and resolved. This means your mutation status will be in a loading state until the promise resolves.

This is how to use the `onSettled` option:

```
useMutation({
  onSettled : (data, error) => console.log("mutation has
    settled"),
});
```

In the snippet, we pass an arrow function to our `onSettled` option. When the mutation fails or succeeds, this function assigned to the `onSettled` option will be called with the thrown error or the resolved data. We then log a message in our console.

By now, you should be familiar with how the `useMutation` hook works and should be able to start using it to create, update, or delete your server state data. Now, let us see how we can leverage this hook and some of its options to perform some common side-effect patterns.

Performing side-effect patterns after mutations

As you read this section title, you might have been wondering whether you've seen how to perform side effects after your mutations previously. The answer is yes, you already did. To perform side effects after a mutation, you can leverage any of these options:

- `onMutate`
- `onSuccess`
- `onError`
- `onSettled`

Now, what you haven't seen is how you can leverage these side effects to do some amazing things that might improve your user experience, such as performing multiple side effects, refetching a query, or even updating your query data after a mutation.

In this section, we will review some ways we leverage the callback functions of our `useMutation` hook and more to perform the previously mentioned side effects.

How to perform an additional side effect

During development, a scenario may come up where it would be useful if you could perform two `onSuccess` callbacks. Now, you can definitely add as much logic as you want to your `useMutation` hook callback, but what if you wanted to split the logic or only execute this specific logic on one single mutation? This would indeed be useful because you could separate the concerns and logic. Well, you can definitely do it!

The `mutate` function allows you to create your own callback functions that will execute after your `useMutation` callbacks.

You just need to be aware that your `useMutation` callbacks run first, and then your `mutate` function callbacks. This is important to know because sometimes if you do something that causes your hook to unmount on your `useMutation` callback, your `mutate` function callbacks might not be called after.

Here is an example of how to use the `mutate` callback functions:

```
const { mutate } = useMutation({
  mutationFn: createUser,
  onSuccess: (data) => {
    showToast(`${data.data.name} was created
      successfuly`)
  }
});

const submitForm = (e) => {
  e.preventDefault()
  mutate({ name }, {
    onSuccess: (data) => {
      const userId = data.data.userID
      goToRoute(`/user/${userId}`)
    }
  })
}
...
```

In the preceding snippet, we leverage the `mutate` callback functions to perform some extra side effects. Here is what we are doing:

1. We create our mutation with `useMutation`.
2. Inside this mutation, we leverage the `onSuccess` callback, which will receive the resolved data and display a toast to the user to let them know that data was created.
3. We then create a `submitForm` function that will be given to an `onSubmit` event later on in our code.
4. When triggered, this function will prevent the received event from propagating.
5. This function will also trigger our mutation by calling `mutate`. In this `mutate`, we leverage its `onSuccess` callback to trigger a route change.

Now that we know how to use the `mutate` callback functions to perform some extra side effects, let's see how we can retrigger a query after performing a mutation.

How to retrigger a query refetch after mutation

When performing mutations that will change the data of a query you are currently displaying to your users, it is recommended that you refetch that query. This is because, at this time, you know that this data has changed, but if your query is still marked as fresh internally, React Query won't refetch it; therefore, you must do it yourself.

Having read the previous two chapters, when you read this section title, something must have come to your mind, and that is query invalidation!

Here is how you can leverage the `onSuccess` callback to retrigger a query refetch:

```
const queryClient = useQueryClient()

const { data } = useQuery({
  queryKey: ["allUsers"],
  queryFn: fetchAllData,
});


const { mutate } = useMutation({
  mutationFn: createUser,
  onSuccess: () => {
    queryClient.invalidateQueries({
      queryKey: ["allUsers"],
    })
  }
});
```

In the preceding snippet, we leverage our `onSuccess` callback to retrigger a query after a successful mutation. Here is what we are doing:

1. We get access to `queryClient`.
2. We create our query with `["allUsers"]` as a query key.
3. We create our mutation. In this mutation `onSuccess` callback, we leverage our `queryClient` `invalidateQueries` method to trigger a refetch of our query with `["allUsers"]` as the query key.

As mentioned at the beginning of this section, this is a recommended practice, and you should do it every time you are mutating data your user sees on the page. Now, you might be thinking: if our mutation was successful, it might have returned the new data, so can't we just manually update our query data and avoid an extra request?

How to perform an update to our query data after a mutation

You can definitely manually update your query data. All you need is access to `queryClient` and the query key of the query you want to update.

While this might be a practice that might save some bandwidth on the user side, it doesn't guarantee that the data you end up displaying to your user is accurate. What if someone else using the same application changes your data?

Now, if there are guarantees that there is no one else able to update this server state, then feel free to try. Just be sure that your query refetches somewhere in between to guarantee that all the data is up to date.

Here is how you can perform an update to your query data after a successful mutation:

```
const queryClient = useQueryClient()

const { data } = useQuery({
  queryKey: ["allUsers"],
  queryFn: fetchAllData,
});

const { mutate } = useMutation({
  mutationFn: createUser,
  onSuccess: (data) => {
    const user = data.data
    queryClient.setQueryData(["allUsers"], (prevData) =>
      [user, ...prevData]);
  }
});
```

In the previous snippet, we leverage our `onSuccess` callback to update our query data and avoid refetching it. Here is what we are doing:

1. We get access to `queryClient`.
2. We create our query with `["allUsers"]` as a query key.

3. We create our mutation. In this mutation `onSuccess` callback, we leverage our `queryClient` `setQueryData` function to manually update the data of the query with `["allUsers"]` as the query key.
4. In this update, we create a new array that combines our created data and our previous data to create the new query data.

As you can see, there are a couple of patterns you can apply to improve your user experience after performing mutations. Now, when speaking about mutations often, one topic shows up every time, which is the topic that will close this chapter: optimistic updates!

Performing optimistic updates

As we saw in *Chapter 2*, an optimistic update is a pattern used during an ongoing mutation where we update our UI to show how it will look after our mutation is finished, although our mutation is still not confirmed as complete.

Well, React Query allows you to perform optimistic updates, and it makes it extremely simple. All you need is to use the callback functions we saw in the previous sections.

Here is how to perform an optimist update using the `useMutation` hook:

```
import axios from "axios";
import { useQuery, useMutation, useQueryClient } from
  "@tanstack/react-query";
import { useState } from "react";

const fetchAllData = async () => {
  const { data } = await axios.get(
    `https://danieljcafonso.builtwithdark.com/name-api`
  );
  return data;
};

const createUser = async (user) => {
  return axios.post
    (`https://danieljcafonso.builtwithdark.com/name-api`,
      user);
};
const Mutation = () => {
  const queryClient = useQueryClient();
```

```js
const [name, setName] = useState("");
const [age, setAge] = useState(0);

const { data } = useQuery({
  queryKey: ["allUsers"],
  queryFn: fetchAllData,
});

const mutation = useMutation({
  mutationFn: createUser,
  onMutate: async (user) => {
    await queryClient.cancelQueries({
      queryKey: ["allUsers"],
    });

    const previousUsers = queryClient.getQueryData({
      queryKey: ["allUsers"],
    });

    queryClient.setQueryData(["allUsers"], (prevData) =>
      [user, ...prevData]);

    return { previousUsers };
  },
  onError: (error, user, context) => {
    showToast("Something went wrong...")
    queryClient.setQueryData(["allUsers"], context.
      previousUsers);
  },
  onSettled: () =>
    queryClient.invalidateQueries({
      queryKey: ["allUsers"],
    }),
});

return (
```

```
    <div>
     {data?.map((user) => (
        <div key={user.userID}>
          Name: {user.name} Age: {user.age}
        </div>
     ))}
      <form>
        <input
          name="name"
          type={"text"}
          onChange={(e) => setName(e.target.value)}
          value={name}
        />
        <input
          name="number"
          type={"number"}
          onChange={(e) => setAge(Number(e.target.value))}
          value={age}
        />
        <button
          type="button"
          onClick={(e) => {
            e.preventDefault()
            mutation.mutate({ name, age })
          }}
        >
          Add
        </button>
      </form>
    </div>
  );
};
```

In the preceding snippet, we put our gained knowledge about mutations into practice to create a better user experience for our users using optimistic updates. Here is what we are doing:

1. We define the needed imports for our code.
2. Create the `fetchAllData` query function. This function will trigger a `GET` request to our endpoint to fetch the user data.
3. Create the `createUser` mutation function. This function will receive the user and perform a `POST` request to our endpoint to create it.
4. Inside our `Mutation` component, we do the following:

    I. We get access to `queryClient`.

    II. Create state variables and respective setters for the name and age inputs.

    III. Create our query using `["allUsers"]` as the query key and `fetchAllData` as the query function.

    IV. Create our mutation using `createUser` as the mutation function. Inside this mutation, we define some callbacks:

    i. On the `onMutate` callback, we do our optimistic update:

    - We make sure we cancel any ongoing queries for our query with `["allUsers"]` as the query key. To do this, we use our `queryClient cancelQueries` method.
    - We save our previous data cached under the `["allUsers"]` query key just in case we need to roll back. To do this, we leverage our `queryClient getQueryData` function.
    - We perform our optimistic update by merging our new data with our previous data and updating the data cached under the `["allUsers"]` query key. To do this, we leverage our `queryClient setQueryData` function.
    - We return our `previousUsers` data in case we need to roll back.

    ii. On the `onError` callback, in case of an error, we need to roll back our data:

    - As a good practice, we let our users know something went wrong with our mutation. In this scenario, we are displaying a toast notification.
    - To do the rollback, we access our context parameter and leverage the `previousUsers` data returned from the `onMutate` callback. We then use this variable to override the cached data under the `["allUsers"]` query key. To do this, we use our `queryClient setQueryData` function.

    iii. On the `onSettled` callback, when our mutation settles, we need to refetch our data:

    - To refetch our data, we leverage our `queryClient invalidateQueries` and invalidate the query with `["allUsers"]` as the query key.

      iv. In our component return, we create a `div` element with the following:

- We use the `data` variable from our query to display our users' data.
- We create our controlled form with our name and age inputs.
- We also create a button that, when pressed, fires its `onClick` event and consequentially triggers our mutation with our name and age values.

Having seen how you build an optimistic update, here is the flow of our created optimistic update:

1. Our component renders, and our query fetches our data and caches it.
2. When we click on the **Add** button, the data returned from the query is automatically updated to include the new user and reflects this change on the UI immediately.
3. If there is an error, we roll back to our previous data.
4. When our mutation settles, we refetch the data for the query we just performed the optimistic update on to ensure our query is updated.

With this knowledge under your belt, you now have all the knowledge you need to take your mutation game to the next level with the help of your new ally: `useMutation`!

Summary

In this chapter, we learned how React Query allows us to perform mutations by using the `useMutation` hook. By now, you should be able to create, delete, or update your server state. To make these changes, you resort to the mutation function, which, like your query function, supports any client and allows you to use GraphQL or REST as long it returns a promise.

You learned about some things the `useMutation` hook returns, such as the `mutate` and `mutateAsync` functions. Similar to `useQuery`, `useMutation` also returns the mutation `data` and `error` variables and gives you access to some statuses you can use to craft a better user experience. For your convenience, `useMutation` also returns a `reset` function to clear your state and an `isPaused` variable in case your mutation enters a paused state.

For you to customize your developer experience, you learned about some commonly used options that allow you to customize your `useMutation` hook experience. We then leveraged four of these options to teach you how to perform some side effects after your mutation runs.

Finally, you used some of the knowledge you learned to perform optimistic updates and craft a better experience for your application users.

In *Chapter 7, Server-Side Rendering with Next.js or Remix*, we'll understand how we can leverage React Query even in a scenario where we are using a server-side framework. You will learn how you can fetch your data in the server and provision React Query on your client side to make it work and craft a better experience.

7
Server-Side Rendering with Next.js or Remix

Not all of our applications are rendered on the client side. Using frameworks that leverage **server-side rendering** (**SSR**) is common nowadays. These frameworks have helped improve application performance, and their adoption is growing daily.

Now, when using these frameworks, most of the time, we tend to perform data fetching or mutations on the server side, which leads to the question:

Do I still need React Query with an SSR framework?

In this chapter, you'll understand how React Query fits with frameworks such as **Next.js** and **Remix** and helps improve your user experience. You will also learn about the two patterns you can apply to React Query with these frameworks: `initialData` and `hydrate`.

Once you are familiar with these patterns, you will see how to apply them to your Next.js and Remix applications.

In this chapter, we'll cover the following topics:

- Why should I use React Query with server-side rendering frameworks?
- Using the `initialData` pattern
- Using the `hydrate` pattern

Technical requirements

All the code examples for this chapter can be found on GitHub at https://github.com/PacktPublishing/State-management-with-React-Query/tree/feat/chapter_7.

Why should I use React Query with server-side rendering frameworks?

SSR has proven to be a good ally to web developers. With an increase in the popularity of full-stack frameworks such as Next.js and, most recently, Remix, the React ecosystem has changed, leading to new patterns being applied.

> **What is server-side rendering (SSR)?**
> SSR is a process that allows you to render your application on the server instead of the browser. During this process, the server sends the rendered page to the client. The client then makes the page fully interactive through a process called hydration.

Owing to the possibility of using SSR, one of the things that might make sense to do is fetch your data on the server. This has many advantages, but one of the best is giving your users their pages with the initial data already loaded. Now, just because you are loading data on the server side doesn't invalidate the scenarios in which you might need to fetch your data on the client side. If your page contains frequently updated data on the client side, React Query continues to be your best friend.

But how does React Query fit within our code using frameworks such as Next.js or Remix? Will we fetch data on the server and then on the client again?

The short answer is no. If we did that, we would just be wasting memory on the server and not leveraging the advantages of SSR. What we can do instead is prefetch our data on the server side and feed it to React Query so that it can manage it on the client side. That way, when the user gets the page, the page will already have the data the user needs, and from that point on, React Query takes care of everything.

We can apply two patterns to prefetch data on the server and send it to React Query on the client side. They are as follows:

- The `initialData` pattern
- The `hydrate` pattern

In the next section, we will learn how to leverage the `initialData` pattern and apply it to the frameworks mentioned: Next.js and Remix.

Using the initialData pattern

The `initialData` pattern is an option you can set in your `useQuery` hook. With this option, you can feed `useQuery` with the data that it will use to initialize a specific query.

This is the process of how to leverage the best of your server-side framework and React Query with the `initialData` option:

1. The first thing you do is prefetch your data on the server side and send it to your component.
2. Inside your component, you render your query using the `useQuery` hook.
3. Inside this hook, you add the `initialData` option and pass the data you prefetched on the server to it.

Let's now see how to use this pattern in Next.js.

Applying the initialData pattern in Next.js

In the following snippet, we will fetch some data on the server using Next.js `getServerSideProps` and then leverage the `initialData` pattern to feed the data to React Query:

```
import axios from "axios";
import { useQuery } from "@tanstack/react-query";

const fetchData = async ({ queryKey }) => {
  const { username } = queryKey[0];
  const { data } = await axios.get(
    `https://danieljcafonso.builtwithdark.com/
      react-query-api/${username}`
  );
  return data;
};

export async function getServerSideProps() {
  const user = await fetchData({ queryKey: [{ username:
    "danieljcafonso" }] });
  return { props: { user } };
}

export default function InitialData (props) {
  const { data } = useQuery({
```

```
    queryKey: [{ queryIdentifier: "api", username:
      "danieljcafonso" }],
    queryFn: fetchData,
    initialData: props.user,
  });

  return <div>This page is server side generated
    {data.hello}</div>;
}
```

In the preceding snippet, we apply the `initialData` pattern to a Next.js application. Here, we have a component that will be server-side-generated. This is what we are doing:

1. We do the necessary imports for this component. In this scenario, it's `axios` and our `useQuery` hook.
2. We create our query function. In this function, we get access to our query key and destructure our username from the query key to perform our `GET` request. We then return our query data.
3. Since we want this page to be server-side-rendered, we include the `getServerSideProps` function in it. This function will run on the server side, and in it, we call our `fetchData` function to get our server state data and return it as props, which will be sent to our `InitialData` component.
4. In our `InitialData` component, we get access to our `props`. In these `props`, we can access the data returned from our `getServerSideProps` function. We then pass this data to our created `useQuery` instance as the `initialData` option. This means this hook will have the data we fetched at build time as its initial data before refetching it.

Now that you know how to apply this pattern in Next.js, let us do it in Remix.

Applying the initialData pattern in Remix

In the following snippet, we will fetch some data on the server using the Remix `loader` and then leverage the `initialData` pattern to feed the data to React Query:

```
import axios from "axios";
import { useQuery } from "@tanstack/react-query";
import { useLoaderData } from "@remix-run/react";
import { json } from "@remix-run/node";

const fetchData = async ({ queryKey }) => {
  const { username } = queryKey[0];
```

```
  const { data } = await axios.get(
    `https://danieljcafonso.builtwithdark.com/
      react-query-api/${username}`
  );
  return data;
};

export async function loader() {
  const user = await fetchData({ queryKey: [{ username:
    "danieljcafonso" }] });
  return json({ user });
}

export default function InitialData() {
  const { user } = useLoaderData();

  const { data } = useQuery({
    queryKey: [{ queryIdentifier: "api", username:
      "danieljcafonso" }],
    queryFn: fetchData,
    initialData: user,
  });

  return <div>This page is server side rendered
    {data.hello}</div>;
}
```

In the preceding snippet, we apply the `initialData` pattern to a Remix application. This is what we are doing here:

1. We do the necessary imports for this component. In this scenario, it's `axios`, our `useQuery` hook, Remix's `useLoaderData` hook, and a `json` function.
2. We create our query function. In this function, we get access to our query key and destructure our username from the query key to perform our `GET` request. We then return our query data.
3. We then create our `loader` function. This is the function Remix uses to allow you to load the data on the server side that will be needed in your components. Inside it, we fetch our data and then use the `json` function to send an `HTTP` response with `application/json` `content-type` as the header and our data included in it.

4. In our `InitialData` component, we leverage `useLoaderData` to get access to the data returned by `loader`. We then pass this data to our created `useQuery` instance as the `initialData` option. This means this hook will have the data we fetched at build time as its initial data before refetching it.

By now, you should be able to use the `initialData` pattern. There are a couple of things you need to be aware of to use it more effectively:

- If you have multiple instances of the same query in different places, you must always pass `initialData` to them. This means that even if you leverage your query at the top level and on a child component, you will have to prop-drill your `initialData` until it reaches the desired component that needs the data.
- Since you fetch the data on the server and pass it to your hook, React Query will base the information it needs to identify when your query was rendered on the initial page load instead of the time at which it was fetched on the server.

Let us now see the second pattern you can leverage when using React Query with server-side-rendered frameworks: the `hydrate` pattern.

Using the hydrate pattern

With the `hydrate` pattern, you can dehydrate your `QueryClient` with a previously prefetched query and send it to your client. On the client side, as soon as the page loads and JavaScript is available, React Query will hydrate your `QueryClient` with the existing data. After this process, React Query will also ensure your queries are up to date.

This is the process of how to leverage the best of your server-side framework and React Query with the `hydrate` pattern:

1. The first thing you do is create a `QueryClient` instance.
2. Using the previously created `QueryClient` instance, you leverage its `prefetchQuery` method to prefetch the data for that given query key.
3. You dehydrate your `QueryClient` and send it to the client side.
4. Your client receives the dehydrated state, hydrates it, and merges it with the `QueryClient` in use.
5. Inside your component, you render your query using the `useQuery` hook with the same query key you added in *step 2*. Your query will already have its data.

In the next section, we will learn how to leverage the `hydrate` pattern and apply it to the frameworks mentioned: Next.js and Remix.

Applying the hydrate pattern in Next.js

Next.js uses the _app component to initialize all your pages and allows you to keep some shared state or persist layouts between page changes. Due to this, we can leverage it to wrap all our components with Hydrate. The `Hydrate` wrapper is responsible for receiving `dehydratedState` and hydrating it.

Let us now see how to apply this wrapper:

```
import { useState } from "react";
import {
  Hydrate,
  QueryClient,
  QueryClientProvider,
} from "@tanstack/react-query";

export default function App({ Component, pageProps }) {
  const [queryClient] = useState(() => new QueryClient());

  return (
    <QueryClientProvider client={queryClient}>
      <Hydrate state={pageProps.dehydratedState}>
        <Component {...pageProps} />{" "}
      </Hydrate>
    </QueryClientProvider>
  );
}
```

In the preceding snippet, we do the following:

1. We do all the necessary imports to set up our components. In this scenario, we get the `useState` function from React and `Hydrate`, `QueryClient`, and `QueryClientProvider` from React Query.
2. Inside our `App` component, we do the following:
   I. We start by creating a new `QueryClient` instance and assigning it as a `state` variable by using the `useState` hook. This is because we need to make sure this data is not shared by different users of our application and requests. This will also make sure we only create `QueryClient` once.

II. We then pass our `queryClient` to `QueryClientProvider` to initiate it and allow it to be accessed by our React Query hooks. `QueryClientProvider` will also wrap our `Component`.

III. Finally, we also wrap our `Component` with `Hydrate`. Since `Hydrate` needs to receive `dehydratedState` whenever it exists, we get `pageProps` from our `App` and pass it to our `Hydrate` state property. This means that for every component that receives `dehydratedState` as props, these props will be passed to our `Hydrate` wrapper.

Now, we are all set to start dehydrating data. Let us see how we can do it:

```
import axios from "axios";
import { dehydrate, QueryClient, useQuery } from
  "@tanstack/react-query";

const fetchData = async ({ queryKey }) => {
  const { username } = queryKey[0];
  const { data } = await axios.get(
    `https://danieljcafonso.builtwithdark.com/
      react-query-api/${username}`
  );
  return data;
};

export async function getServerSideProps() {
  const queryClient = new QueryClient();
  await queryClient.prefetchQuery(
    [{ queryIdentifier: "api", username: "danieljcafonso" }],
    fetchData
  );

  return { props: { dehydratedState: dehydrate(queryClient) }
};
}

export default function SSR() {
  const { data } = useQuery({
    queryKey: [{ queryIdentifier: "api", username:
      "danieljcafonso" }],
```

```
    queryFn: fetchData,
  });

  return <div>This page is server-side-rendered
    {data.hello}</div>;
}
```

In the preceding snippet, we prefetch some data, which will be dehydrated and then hydrated by React Query. Here is what we are doing:

1. We do the necessary imports for this component. In this scenario, it's axios, and from the React Query side, the dehydrate function, QueryClient, and the useQuery hook.
2. We create our query function. In this function, we get access to our query key, and destructure our username from the query key to perform our GET request. We then return our query data.
3. In getServerSideProps, we do the following:
    I. We create a new QueryClient instance.
    II. We then leverage the previously created instance to prefetch a query that will be cached under the [{ queryIdentifier: "api", username: "danieljcafonso" }] query key and use fetchData as the query function.
    III. We use dehydrate on queryClient and return it as props so it can be picked up in our App component.
4. In our SSR component, we create a useQuery hook with [{ queryIdentifier: "api", username: "danieljcafonso" }] as the query key and fetchData as the query function.

Given that we returned dehydratedState from our getServerSideProps function, this will be passed as pageProps and picked up by the Hydrate wrapper wrapping our component. This means that React Query will pick up our dehydrated state, hydrate it, and merge this new data with the current data in QueryClient. This means that when the hook inside SSR first runs, it will already have the data prefetched from getServerSidePros.

Now that you know how to apply this pattern to Next.js, let us do it in Remix.

Applying the hydrate pattern in Remix

Remix uses the root component to define the root layout of all your pages and to allow you to keep some shared state between page changes. The way this is done is by using the Outlet component. Due to this component and Outlet at the root level, we can leverage it to wrap all our components with Hydrate.

Now, unlike Next.js, there is no way to access `pageProps` to access `dehydratedState` at the root level. Therefore, we need to install a third-party package called `use-dehydrated-state`.

Here is how to add `use-dehydrated-state` to your project:

- If you are running npm in your project, run the following command:

    ```
    npm i use-dehydrated-state
    ```

- If you are using Yarn, run the following command:

    ```
    yarn add use-dehydrated-state
    ```

- If you are using pnpm, run the following command:

    ```
    pnpm add use-dehydrated-state
    ```

`use-dehydrated-state` allows us to access our dehydrated state at our root-level component.

Now, we can do the necessary setup to leverage the `Hydrate` and `QueryClientProvider` wrappers:

```
import {
  ...
  Outlet,
} from "@remix-run/react";
import { useState } from "react";
import {
  Hydrate,
  QueryClient,
  QueryClientProvider,
} from "@tanstack/react-query";
import { useDehydratedState } from "use-dehydrated-state";

export default function App() {
  const [queryClient] = useState(() => new QueryClient());
  const dehydratedState = useDehydratedState();

  return (
    ...
        <QueryClientProvider client={queryClient}>
          <Hydrate state={dehydratedState}>
            <Outlet />
```

```
        </Hydrate>
      </QueryClientProvider>
      ...
  );
}
```

In the preceding snippet, we do the following:

1. We do all the necessary imports to set up our components. In this scenario, we get the following:

    I. Remix's `Outlet`

    II. The `useState` function from React

    III. `Hydrate`, `QueryClient`, and `QueryClientProvider` from React Query

    IV. The `useDehydratedState` hook from `use-dehydrated-state`

2. Inside our `App` component, we do the following:

    I. We start by creating a new `QueryClient` instance and assigning it as a `state` variable by using the `useState` hook. This is because we need to make sure this data is not shared by different users of our application and requests. This will also make sure we only create `QueryClient` once.

    II. We then pass our `queryClient` to `QueryClientProvider` to initiate it and allow it to be accessed by our React Query hooks. `QueryClientProvider` will also wrap the component rendered by `Outlet`.

    III. Finally, we also wrap `Outlet` with `Hydrate`. Since `Hydrate` needs to receive `dehydratedState` whenever it is received from the server, we get it from the `useDehydratedState` hook. This means that for every component that receives `dehydratedState` from its `loader`, this data will be passed to our `Hydrate` wrapper.

Now, we are all set to start dehydrating data. Let us see how to do it:

```
import axios from "axios";
import { dehydrate, QueryClient, useQuery } from "@tanstack/
react-query";
import { json } from "@remix-run/node";

const fetchData = async ({ queryKey }) => {
  const { username } = queryKey[0];
  const { data } = await axios.get(
    `https://danieljcafonso.builtwithdark.com/
```

```
        react-query-api/${username}`
  );
  return data;
};

export async function loader() {
  const queryClient = new QueryClient();
  await queryClient.prefetchQuery(
    [{ queryIdentifier: "api", username: "danieljcafonso" }],
    fetchData
  );
  return json({ dehydratedState: dehydrate(queryClient) });
}

export default function Index() {
  const { data } = useQuery({
    queryKey: [{ queryIdentifier: "api", username:
      "danieljcafonso" }],
    queryFn: fetchData,
  });

  return <div>This page is server side rendered
    {data.hello}</div>;
}
```

In the preceding snippet, we are prefetching some data, which will be dehydrated and then hydrated by React Query. Here is what we are doing:

1. We do the necessary imports for this component. In this scenario, they are as follows:

    I. The `axios` client

    II. The `dehydrate` function, `QueryClient`, and the `useQuery` hook from the React Query side

    III. The `json` function from Remix

2. We create our query function. In this function, we get access to our query key and destructure our username from the query key to perform our `GET` request. We then return our query data.

3. In `loader`, we do the following:

I. We create a new `QueryClient` instance.

II. We then leverage the previously created instance to prefetch a query that will be cached under the `[{ queryIdentifier: "api", username: "danieljcafonso" }]` query key and use `fetchData` as the query function.

III. We then use `dehydrate` for `queryClient` and return it as an HTTP response.

4. In our `Index` component, we create a `useQuery` hook with `[{ queryIdentifier: "api", username: "danieljcafonso" }]` as the query key and `fetchData` as the query function.

Given that we returned `dehydratedState` from our `loader` function, this will be picked up by `useDehydratedState` and passed to our `Hydrate` wrapper, wrapping our component. This means that React Query will pick up `dehydratedState`, hydrate it, and merge this new data with the current data in `QueryClient`. Due to this process, when the hook inside `Index` first runs, it will already have the data that we prefetched from `loader`.

Summary

This chapter taught us how React Query can complement our server-side-rendered applications.

You learned how React Query enables you to prefetch data on the server and send it to React Query on the client side. To do this, you got to know two patterns, `initialData` and `hydrate`. In the `initialData` pattern, you prefetch the data on the server and pass it to the `initialData` option in the `useQuery` hook on the client side. In the `hydrate` pattern, you prefetch your query on the server, dehydrate the query cache, and hydrate it on the client side.

In *Chapter 8, Testing React Query Hooks and Components*, we will focus on one of the things that will help you sleep better at night: testing. You will get to know how you can test your component, that is, using React Query, as well as some custom hooks for improving your developer experience.

8
Testing React Query Hooks and Components

You have almost mastered React Query! By now, you are well aware of how queries and mutations work and are ready to leverage React Query in a server-side, rendered project as well. Now, we'll look at the last skill you need to be a full-on React Query hero – testing React Query using code.

This chapter will teach you how to test your `useQuery` and `useMutation` using components and hooks. But before that, you will get to know a super useful library to help you test your React Query code called Mock Service Worker.

You will then learn some restructuring tips and tricks you can leverage to make your React Query code more readable and reusable.

With this knowledge, you can start testing your code. You will start with testing your components that leverage React Query and see what testing from a user-centric approach looks like for queries and mutations.

Finally, we will dive into implementation details and see when and how we should test our hooks that use React Query.

In this chapter, we'll be covering the following topics:

- Configuring Mock Service Worker
- Organizing code
- Testing components that use React Query
- Testing custom hooks that use React Query

Technical requirements

All the code examples for this chapter can be found on GitHub at `https://github.com/PacktPublishing/State-management-with-React-Query/tree/feat/chapter_8`.

Configuring Mock Service Worker

When testing React applications, one question often asked is how to test API calls. This question often leads to a follow-up question: *"How can I make sure my network requests return the data I expect so that my tests always receive the same data and don't become flaky?"* There are many ways to answer these questions, and many implementations we can follow. The most common implementation often leveraged is mocking your data-fetching clients.

While this approach works, one thing that I've seen often in all the projects that I have worked on that followed this method is that the more tests you write, the more unmaintainable they become. This is due to the fact that mocking things such as `fetch` or `axios` comes with a lot of boilerplate code to take care of things such as different routes being hit, different responses for the same route, and cleaning up your client mocks to avoid tests leaking on each other. Let us not forget that if we use GraphQL and REST in the same application, we must mock an extra client, depending on the component you are testing.

What if I told you there is an alternative you can use to intercept your network requests and return predefined data without having to mock any client? What if I told you this alternative supports REST and GraphQL? What if I told you that this alternative could also be used in your application to provide some dummy data for a route your backend team has not yet implemented? You can do all this with **Mock Service Worker** (**MSW**).

As the MSW docs say: *"Mock Service Worker is an API mocking library that uses Service Worker API to intercept actual requests"* (`https://mswjs.io/docs/`).

MSW leverages service workers to intercept requests on the network level and return some predefined data for that specific request. This means that just by having a defined API contract, you can return mocked data even before that endpoint exists. Also, leveraging this predefined data in your tests means you no longer need to mock `axios` or `fetch`. It is important to mention that service workers only work in the browser. In your tests, MSW uses a request interceptor library to allow you to reuse the same mock definitions you have in your browser.

While leveraging MSW in the browser is super helpful, it sits outside this chapter's scope. In this chapter, we will only use MSW in our tests.

Here is how to add MSW to your project:

- If you are running npm in your project, run the following command:

    ```
    npm install msw --save-dev
    ```

- If you are using Yarn, run the following command:

  ```
  yarn add msw --dev
  ```

- If you are using pnpm, run the following command:

  ```
  pnpm add msw --save-dev
  ```

Once MSW is installed, we must create our request handlers and response resolvers.

Request handlers allow you to specify the method, path, and response when handling a request. They are often paired with response resolvers. A response resolver is a function you pass to the request handler that allows you to specify the mocked response when intercepting a request.

Let us now create some handlers to handle some routes. Here is what we have to do.

Inside the `src/mocks` folder, create a `handlers.js` file.

In the `handlers.js` file, add the following code:

```
import { rest } from "msw";

export const handlers = [
  rest.get("*/api/*", (req, res, ctx) => {
    return res(
      ctx.status(200),
      ctx.json({
        data: "value"
      })
    );
  }),
];
```

In the preceding snippet, we do the following:

1. We import the `rest` namespace containing a set of request handlers to handle REST requests.
2. We create a `handlers` array that will contain all of our request handlers.

   The first mock we create is for a GET request to any route that contains `/api/`.

   When a request hits this request handler, it will return a response that will, in turn, return a 200 OK response code with an object that, inside the `data` property, will include a `"value"` string.

Now that we have created our `handlers`, we need to ensure that MSW will intercept our requests using our previously created `handlers`.

This is what we have to do.

Inside the `src/mocks` folder, create a `server.js` file.

In the `server.js` file, add the following code:

```
import { setupServer } from "msw/node";
import { handlers } from "./handlers";

export const server = setupServer(...handlers);
```

In the preceding snippet, we leverage the `setupServer` function and our created `handlers` array to create an object responsible for intercepting our requests with our given `handlers`.

Now that we have created our server file, we need to ensure `Jest` uses them. To do this, inside our `setupTests.js` file, add the following code:

```
import { server } from "./mocks/server.js";

beforeAll(() => server.listen());
afterEach(() => server.resetHandlers());
afterAll(() => server.close());
```

This is what we do in the preceding snippet:

1. We import our created `server` object.
2. We leverage the `beforeAll` global hook to ensure that MSW is intercepting our requests before any of our tests are executed.
3. We then leverage the `afterEach` global hook so that after every single test, we reset our handlers. This considers a scenario where we add a custom handler for one of our tests so that they don't leak into another test.
4. Finally, we leverage the `afterAll` global hook so that after all our tests run, we clean up and stop intercepting requests.

Now, any API requests made by our tests will be intercepted by MSW.

Before seeing how we can test our components and React Query using hooks, let us see a couple of patterns we can apply to make our code more structured and easier to test.

Organizing code

There are many ways you can organize your code. Now, one thing we need to be aware of is choosing patterns that save you some time and make your code better in the long run. This section will discuss three different patterns that we can leverage together or independently to make our code more structured, readable, and organized. Here's what we will discuss in this section:

- Creating an API file
- Leveraging query key factories
- Creating a hooks folder

Creating an API file

Creating an API file to contain all my requests for a specific domain is a pattern that I follow.

In this file, I leverage my API client and create the functions responsible to make a request to a given route and return the request data.

This is particularly useful because it avoids repeating the logic for the same request in your code and focuses all the domain-specific requests in the same file.

For all the requests made in the scope of this book, I would prefer to create a file for my user domain, given that the scope seems to be focused on users. So, inside our `api` folder, we will create a `userAPI.js` file.

Figure 8.1 – Adding userAPI.js to our API folder

Inside that file, we can now move all of our requests inside our code. This is how it might look:

```
import axios from "axios";

export const axiosInstance = axios.create({
  baseURL: "https://danieljcafonso.builtwithdark.com",
});

export const getUser = async (username, signal) => {
  const { data } = await axiosInstance.get
    (`/react-query-api/${username}`, {
    signal,
```

```
  });
  return data;
};

export const createUser = async (user) => {
  return axiosInstance.post(`/name-api`, user);
};
```

In the preceding snippet, we can see an example of a `userAPI` file containing our `axios` client instance, a `getUser` function (to fetch data from a given user), and a `createUser` function (to create a user).

As you can see, this pattern improves the code reusability and readability in the components that end up using the functions from our API file.

One extra thing you can do that we didn't do in the preceding snippet is add the specific logic from your query functions. This makes these functions more accessible in your application if you only use React Query. I prefer to keep my query functions and these API functions separated because I often use different query functions with the same API function. Still, it will improve your code readability if you choose to use it.

Leveraging query key factories

Managing query keys is often a nuisance. We forget which ones we have already used and need to go through most of our queries to remember them. This is where query key factories shine.

A query key factory can be a single object that, inside each property, will include a function responsible for generating a query key. This way, you keep all your query keys in the same place and stop wasting time trying to remember them.

This is what your query key factory can look like:

```
export const userKeys = {
    all: () => ["allUsers"],
    api: () => [{queryIdentifier: "api"}],
    withUsername: (username = "username") =>
      [{ ...userKeys.api[0], username }],
    paginated: (page) => [{ ...userKeys.api, page }]
}
```

As you can see from the preceding snippet, we create a `userKey` object, which will be our query key factory. In each property, we have a function that will be responsible for returning our query key.

Creating a hooks folder

The name here also speaks for itself. One recommendation for organizing code I like to follow is creating a hooks folder.

I like to create custom hooks in this folder that contain some of the queries and mutations I often repeat, or ones that end up having too much logic and impact my code readability. This makes it easier for me to test a specific hook in isolation and make the components that use them more readable.

For instance, remember when we performed optimistic updates in *Chapter 6*? The useMutation hook we created is a great candidate to move to a custom hook. I will create a useOptimisticUpdateUserCreation custom hook and move my code in there. This is what that hook will look like:

```
import { useMutation, useQueryClient } from
  "@tanstack/react-query";
import { userKeys } from "../utils/queryKeyFactories";
import { createUser } from "../api/userAPI";

const useOptimisticUpdateUserCreation = () => {
  const queryClient = useQueryClient();

  return useMutation({
    mutationFn: createUser,
    retry: 0,
    onSettled: () => queryClient.invalidateQueries
      (userKeys.all()),
    onMutate: async (user) => {
      await queryClient.cancelQueries(userKeys.all());

      const previousUsers = queryClient.getQueryData
        (userKeys.all());

      queryClient.setQueryData(userKeys.all(), (prevData)
        => [
        user,
        ...prevData,
      ]);
```

```
      return { previousUsers };
    },
    onError: (error, user, context) => {
      queryClient.setQueryData(userKeys.all(),
        context.previousUsers);
    },
  });
};

export default useOptimisticUpdateUserCreation;
```

In the preceding snippet, we create the `useOptimisticUpdateUserCreation` hook and move the code from our `OptimisticMutation` component there. As you can also see from the code, we already applied our API file and query factory pattern.

In the component using our hook, all we have to do now is import the hook and use it like this:

```
const mutation = useOptimisticUpdateUserCreation();
```

Applying all the patterns of this section, this is what your project structure can end up looking like:

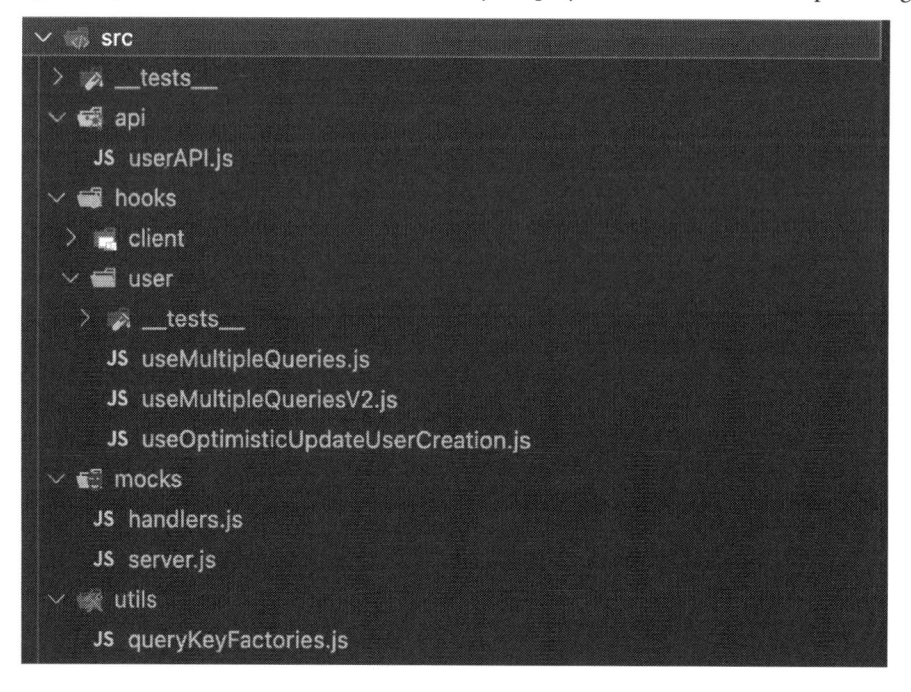

```
v  src
  >  __tests__
  v  api
       JS  userAPI.js
  v  hooks
    >  client
    v  user
      >  __tests__
         JS  useMultipleQueries.js
         JS  useMultipleQueriesV2.js
         JS  useOptimisticUpdateUserCreation.js
  v  mocks
       JS  handlers.js
       JS  server.js
  v  utils
       JS  queryKeyFactories.js
```

Figure 8.2 – What the project structure may look like after following these three patterns

Now that we've seen these patterns, let us finally move to start testing our code. We'll start with one of the most recommended approaches – testing components using React Query hooks.

Testing components that use React Query

When the React Testing Library was first introduced, it was under a main guiding principle that changed how we wrote tests going forward. That guiding principle is, *"The more your tests resemble the way your software is used, the more confidence they can give you"* (https://testing-library.com/docs/guiding-principles/).

From that point on, many things changed in our tests. Focusing on a user-centric approach meant avoiding implementation details in our tests at all costs. This meant no more shallow rendering, no more state and prop references, and a more user-centric way of querying the DOM.

Reading the last paragraph, you might be wondering how to test your components following a user-centric approach. Well, the answer is straightforward – a user doesn't have to know the page they are using leverages React Query. If you write your tests like you are just using the page, this means that you will find issues that your user might find as well accidentally, and if for some reason you change your implementation, your tests won't break.

There will be some scenarios where you might have to tie your tests to some implementation details to help you do some assertions, but we will try to avoid them at all costs in this section.

Before we start writing our tests, we need to do some setting up.

Setting up testing utils

When testing components that leverage React Query, we must ensure we wrap up those components with our `QueryClientProvider`. Now, we could create a custom wrapper for each test and wrap our component with it when rendering, but remember that you will most likely end up with many components that will use React Query in some way.

This is where setting up some testing utils will help you. A pattern that I really like to follow is overwriting the `render` function from the testing library and wrapping every component that is rendered, using this function automatically with our React Query `QueryClientProvider`. To do that, I create a `test-utils.js` file inside a `utils` folder.

This is what we can add to our `test-utils.js` file:

```
import { render } from "@testing-library/react";
import { QueryClient, QueryClientProvider } from
  "@tanstack/react-query";

const customRender = (ui, { ...options } = {}) => {
```

```
  const queryClient = new QueryClient({
    logger: {
      log: console.log,
      warn: console.warn,
      error: () => {},
    },
    defaultOptions: {
      queries: {
        retry: 0,
        cacheTime: Infinity,
      },
    },
  });

  const CombinedProviders = ({ children }) => {
    return (
      <QueryClientProvider client={queryClient}>
        {children}</QueryClientProvider>
    );
  };
  return render(ui, { wrapper: CombinedProviders,
      ...options });
};

export * from "@testing-library/react";
export { customRender as render };
```

This is what we do in the preceding snippet:

1. We import the `render` function from the React Testing Library.
2. We import our `QueryClient` and our `QueryClientProvider` from React Query.
3. We create a custom `render` function (`customRender`):
    I. This function will receive a `ui` parameter, which will be the component we want to render. It will also receive an `options` object, which we can forward to the `render` function.

II. We create our `queryClient` instance. Here, we override our `logger error` property to avoid showing up errors from React Query. This is because we might want to test error scenarios, and we don't want React Query to pollute our `console` with the errors we expect. We also define our queries to never attempt to retry a query after it fails, and we set our `cacheTime` to `Infinity` to avoid `Jest` error messages in scenarios where we manually set a `cacheTime` value.

III. We create a `CombinedProviders` wrapper that will be responsible for wrapping our components with our `QueryClientProvider`.

IV. We call the React Testing Library `render` function, pass it the `ui` parameter, wrap it with our `CombinedProviders`, and send it the `options` we received.

4. We export all of the React Testing Library and our `customRender` function, which will now be the main `render` function. This means we now import this file instead of the React Testing Library in our tests.

Note in the snippet that we create our `queryClient` inside the `customRender` function instead of outside it. You can follow this approach if you want to avoid having to clean up the query cache between tests. If you want to have the same `QueryClient` between tests, you can create the `queryClient` instance outside the function.

Now that our `render` function is ready to render React Query using components, we can start writing tests.

Testing queries

In the following subsections, we will see some common testing scenarios you might find in your day-to-day activities when using React Query.

Checking whether data is fetched

One of the most common tests we have to write is ensuring that our data was fetched properly. Let us start with this scenario and revisit our parallel queries example from *Chapter 5*. We will also rewrite the code to adjust to some of the practices mentioned in this chapter. Let's start by looking at our `ParallelQueries` component:

```
export const ParallelQueries = () => {
  const { multipleQueries } = useMultipleQueriesV2();

  return (
    <div>
      {multipleQueries.map(({ data, isFetching }, index) => (
        <p key={index}>{isFetching ? "Fetching data..." :
```

```
            data.hello}</p>
        ))}
      </div>
    );
};
```

As you can see from the preceding snippet, the code is pretty much the same as the one presented in *Chapter 5,* with the exception of the part where we fetch our data. Here, we applied one of the patterns mentioned in this chapter and moved this logic to a custom hook inside our custom hooks folder.

Let us now look at what sits inside our `useMultipleQueriesV2` hook file:

```
import { useQueries } from "@tanstack/react-query";
import { userKeys } from "../utils/queryKeyFactories";
import { getUser } from "../api/userAPI";

const fetchData = async ({ queryKey }) => {
  const { username } = queryKey[0];
  return await getUser(username);
};

const usernameList = ["userOne", "userTwo", "userThree"];

const useMultipleQueriesV2 = () => {
  const multipleQueries = useQueries({
    queries: usernameList.map((username) => {
      return {
        queryKey: userKeys.withUsername(username),
        queryFn: fetchData,
      };
    }),
  });

  return { multipleQueries }
};

export default useMultipleQueriesV2
```

As you can see from the preceding snippet, we basically just move what we had in our component to our `useMultipleQueriesV2` hook. Note also that we leverage the other two patterns we mentioned in this chapter:

- We create an entry inside the `userKeys` factory and leverage it to set our `useQueries` hook, `queryKey`
- We create an API file to gather our user API functions and add our `getUser` function

This is what our `getUser` function looks like:

```
export const getUser = async (username, signal) => {
  const { data } = await axiosInstance.get
    (`/react-query-api/${username}`, {
    signal,
  });
  return data;
};
```

The `getUser` function shown in this snippet is responsible for making a GET request for our given endpoint and aborting that request if our `signal` tells `axios` to do so.

Now that you are reacquainted with this component and how it works, let's start to test it.

The first thing we need to do before we write our test is to make sure we have MSW intercepting the GET request and returning the data we want:

```
    rest.get("*/react-query-api/*", (req, res, ctx) => {
      return res(
        ctx.delay(500),
        ctx.status(200),
        ctx.json({
          hello: req.params[1],
        })
      );
    })
```

In the preceding snippet, we create a request handler to add to our `handlers` array, which does the following.

Whenever we intercept a GET request to an endpoint that includes the `/react-query-api/` path, we return a `200 OK` response that will be delayed by 500 milliseconds, and it will have in its body an object with a `hello` property that will contain the parameter in the second position of the request parameters.

This means that a GET request for the `https://danieljcafonso.builtwithdark.com/react-query-api/userOne` endpoint will return a `200 OK` response with the following object:

```
{
  hello: "Hello userOne"
}
```

Now that we are sure that our components will always receive the same data after a request, we can write our tests.

Now, I suggest you look at the `ParallelQueries` component from a user-centric perspective and consider the scenarios you might want to test. The rule of thumb here is to think, *"If I was a user interacting with this code, what would I interact with or expect to happen?"*

Following the preceding analysis, I came up with two test scenarios:

- **As a user, I want to see the data my parallel queries fetched**: In this scenario, we want our component to be rendered and wait for it to render a hello message for `userOne`, `userTwo`, and `userThree`.

- **As a user, I want to have a loading indicator being displayed while I have no data**: In this scenario, we want our component to be rendered, and while we wait for our data to be fetched, we should see a `"Fetching data..."` message for each of our requests.

With those scenarios in mind, we can write our tests. Let us see what our test file would look like:

```
import { ParallelQueries } from "../MultipleQueries";
import { render, screen } from "../utils/test-utils";

describe("Parallel Queries Tests", () => {
  test("component should fetch and render multiple data",
    async () => {
      render(<ParallelQueries />);
      const text = await screen.findByText("userOne");
      expect(text).toBeInTheDocument();
      expect(screen.getByText("userTwo")).toBeInTheDocument();
      expect(screen.getByText("userThree")).toBeInTheDocument();
    });
```

```
  test("component should show loading indicator for each
    query", () => {
    render(<ParallelQueries />);
    const isFetching = screen.getAllByText("Fetching data...");
    expect(isFetching).toHaveLength(3);
  });
});
```

Let us now review what we do in the preceding snippet:

1. We import our `ParallelQueries` component and, from our `test-utils`, our custom `render` function and the `screen` object.
2. We create our test suite and, inside it, our tests:

    I. For the `"component should fetch and render multiple data"` test, we do the following:

    i. Render our `ParallelQueries` component.

    ii. Since we need to wait for the data to be fetched, we leverage an `async` query variant (`findBy`) from the React Testing Library and `await` until the `userOne` text shows up on the DOM.

    iii. Once our query finds the `userOne` text, we assert that it is in the DOM and repeat the same assertion for `userTwo` and `userThree`. In these last two examples (`userTwo` and `userThree`), we won't need to leverage the `findBy` variant because the data will already be on the DOM, so we use the `getBy` variant instead.

    II. For the `"component should show loading indicator for each query"` test, we do the following:

    i. Render our `ParallelQueries` component.

    ii. Due to the 500 millisecond delay we added to our mocked response, we won't have our data immediately available to be rendered, so we should have our loading indicators showing up instead. Since we will have multiple indicators, we leverage the `getAllBy` variant to get an array of elements that match our query.

    iii. We then assert that our array of elements has a length of 3 to ensure that we have a `"Fetching data..."` message for each query.

With these tests, we have followed an approach that reflects our user behavior when interacting with our component and, at the same time, got 100% coverage on our `ParallelQueries` component and our `useMultipleQueriesV2` custom hook.

In most scenarios, to deal with data-fetching scenarios, you only need to wait for the data you fetch to be rendered on the DOM. Got a single query? Wait for the data to be displayed on the DOM. Got some parallel queries? Wait for the data to be displayed on the DOM. Got some dependent queries? Wait for the first query data to be displayed on the DOM. Then, repeat this step for the following queries.

Now, in some scenarios, you will have to fire some actions to get to your test assertion. Some of those scenarios might even involve query invalidation or query cancelation. Due to the similarity of these scenarios, let us now see what we can test with query invalidation.

Checking whether a query was invalidated

As you should remember from *Chapter 5*, query invalidation is when you manually mark your query as stale so that React Query can refetch it if it is being rendered.

Let us review the `QueryInvalidation` component we saw in *Chapter 5*:

```
const fetchData = async ({ queryKey}) => {
  const { username } = queryKey[0];
  return await getUser(username);
};

const QueryInvalidation = () => {
  const { data, isFetching } = useQuery({
    queryKey: userKeys.withUsername("userOne"),
    queryFn: fetchData,
  });
  const queryClient = useQueryClient();
  return (
    <div>
      <p>{isFetching ? "Loading..." : data?.hello}</p>
      <button onClick={() => queryClient.invalidateQueries
        (userKeys.api())}>
        Invalidate Query
      </button>
    </div>
  );
};
```

As you can see from the preceding snippet, the code is still very similar to the one from *Chapter 5*. The only changes we made here were to apply the API file pattern and leverage the `getUser` function we saw previously in this chapter and change our query key to leverage the query key factory pattern.

Now that you are reacquainted with this component and how it works, let us start to test it.

As we are leveraging our `getUser` function, we don't need to create a new request handler in MSW due to the fact we are using the same endpoint.

Now, looking at the `QueryInvalidation` component from a user-centric perspective, here are the three test scenarios that you might identify:

- **As a user, I want to see the data my query fetched**: In this scenario, we want our component to be rendered and wait for it to render a hello message for `userOne`.
- **As a user, I want to have a loading indicator displaying while my data is being fetched**: In this scenario, we want our component to be rendered, and when our data is not being fetched, we should see a `"Loading..."` message.
- **As a user, I want my query to be refetched when I click the Invalidate Query button**: In this scenario, we want our component to be rendered, and we wait for it to render a hello message, click the **Invalidate Query** button, wait for the hello message to disappear, wait for the loading indicator to disappear, and wait for the hello message to reappear. This way, we are sure our query was invalidated.

With those scenarios in mind, we can write our tests for our `QueryInvalidation` component. Let us see what our test file would look like:

```
import { QueryInvalidation } from "../QueryClientExamples";
import { fireEvent, render, screen, waitFor } from "../utils/test-utils";

describe("QueryInvalidation Tests", () => {
  test("component should display fetched data", async () => {
    render(<QueryInvalidation />);
    const text = await screen.findByText("userOne");
    expect(text).toBeInTheDocument();
  });

  test("component should show a loading indicator", () => {
    render(<QueryInvalidation />);
    expect(screen.getByText("Loading...")).toBeInTheDocument();
  });
```

```js
test("component should invalidate query", async () => {
  render(<QueryInvalidation />);

  const text = await screen.findByText("userOne");
  expect(text).toBeInTheDocument();

  const invalidateButton = screen.getByRole("button", {
    text: "Invalidate Query",
  });
  fireEvent.click(invalidateButton);

  await waitFor(() =>
    expect(screen.queryByText("userOne")).not.
      toBeInTheDocument()
  );
  await waitFor(() =>
    expect(screen.queryByText("Loading"...")).not.
      toBeInTheDocument()
  );

  expect(screen.getByText("userOne")).
    toBeInTheDocument();
});
});
```

Let us now review what we are doing in the preceding snippet:

1. We import our `QueryInvalidation` component, and from our `test-utils`, we import our custom `render` function, the `screen` object, the `fireEvent` util, and the `waitFor` function.
2. We create our test suite, and inside it, our tests:
    I. For the `"component should display fetched data"` test, we do the following:
       i. Render our `QueryInvalidation` component.
       ii. Since we need to wait for the data to be fetched, we leverage an `async` query variant (`findBy`) from the React Testing Library and `await` until the `userOne` text shows up on the DOM.

iii. Once our query finds the `userOne` text, we assert it is in the DOM.

II. For the `"component should show a loading indicator"` test, we do the following:

i. Render our `QueryInvalidation` component.

ii. Due to the 500 millisecond delay we added to our mocked response, we won't have our data immediately available to be rendered, so we should have our loading indicators showing up instead. We then leverage a `getBy` query variant to help assert that the `"Loading..."` text is in the DOM.

III. For the `"component should invalidate query"` test, we do the following:

i. Render our `QueryInvalidation` component.

ii. We wait for our data to be fetched and consequently assert it is on the DOM.

iii. We find our **Invalidate Query** button by leveraging the `getByRole` query that will help us find the button with the `Invalidate Query` text.

iv. We then leverage the `fireEvent` util to fire a `click` event on our button.

v. We then leverage the `waitFor` function to wait until an assertion evaluates to `true`. In this scenario, we wait for our query data to disappear from the DOM.

vi. We then leverage the `waitFor` function once again, this time to wait for the loading indicator to disappear from the DOM.

vii. Finally, we assert that our query has finished refetching by checking whether our data is back on the DOM again.

Now, we have checked how we can test query invalidation. You might be wondering how query cancelation differs from query invalidation. At the end of the day, testing query cancelation would differ on the following things:

- Our query function would need to receive the `AbortController` signal and forward it to our `getUser` function.
- Instead of calling the `invalidateQuery` function from `queryClient`, we call `cancelQueries`.
- In our tests, the first two scenarios are exactly the same. In the third scenario, we immediately click the **cancel** button after rendering the component. After doing this, the DOM should not show either the data or the loading indicator.

Now that you know how to test most scenarios in a user-centric approach, let's put this knowledge to the test and see how we would test a paginated scenario.

Testing paginated queries

In *Chapter 5*, we learned how `useQuery` allowed us to create paginated queries and consequently used it to build a paginated UI component.

Let us review the `PaginatedQuery` component we saw in *Chapter 5*:

```
import { useQuery } from "@tanstack/react-query";
import { useState } from "react";
import { getPaginatedData } from "./api/userAPI";
import { userKeys } from "./utils/queryKeyFactories";

const fetchData = async ({ queryKey }) => {
  const { page } = queryKey[0];
  return await getPaginatedData(page);
};

const PaginatedQuery = () => {
  const [page, setPage] = useState(0);

  const { isLoading, isError, error, data, isFetching,
    isPreviousData } =
    useQuery({
      queryKey: userKeys.paginated(page),
      queryFn: fetchData,
      keepPreviousData: true,
    });

  if (isLoading) {
  return <h2>Loading initial data...</h2>;
  }

  if (isError) {
    return <h2>{error.message}</h2>;
  }

  return (
    <>
```

```
      <div>
        {data.results.map((user) => (
          <div key={user.email}>
            {user.name.first}
            {user.name.last}
          </div>
        ))}
      </div>
      <div>
        <button
          onClick={() => setPage((oldValue) =>
            Math.max(oldValue - 1, 0))}
          disabled={page === 0}
        >
          Previous Page
        </button>
        <button
          disabled={isPreviousData}
          onClick={() => setPage((old) => old + 1)}
        >
          Next Page
        </button>
      </div>
      {isFetching ? <span> Loading...</span> : null}
    </>
  );
};

export default PaginatedQuery;
```

As you can see from the preceding snippet, it is pretty much the same as what we saw in *Chapter 5*. Note also that we leveraged two patterns we mentioned in this chapter:

- We created an entry into our `userKeys` factory and leveraged it to set our `useQuery` hook, `queryKey`
- We created an API file to gather our user API functions and added our `getPaginatedData` function

This is what our `getPaginatedData` function looks like:

```
export const getPaginatedData = async (page) => {
  const { data } = await axiosInstance.get(
    `/react-query-paginated?page=${page}&results=10`
  );
  return data;
};
```

The `getPaginatedData` function shown in the preceding snippet is responsible for making a GET request for our given endpoint for a given page.

Now that you are reacquainted with this component and how it works, let's test it.

We will start by creating our MSW request handler:

```
rest.get("*/react-query-paginated", (req, res, ctx) => {
    const page = req.url.searchParams.get("page");
    const pageOneData = {
      email: "email1",
      name: {
        first: "first1",
        last: "last1",
      },
    };
    const pageTwoData = {
      email: "email2",
      name: {
        first: "first2",
        last: "last2",
      },
    };
    const data = {
      results: [page > 0 ? pageTwoData : pageOneData],
    };

    return res(ctx.status(200), ctx.json(data));
})
```

In the preceding snippet, we create a request handler to add to our `handlers` array, which does the following.

Whenever we intercept a `GET` request to an endpoint that includes the `/react-query-paginated` path, we get the `page` query parameter to help us define what data we will return.

We return a `200 OK` response that will have in its body an object with the data for page one or page two, depending on the received page query parameter.

This means that a `GET` request for the `https://danieljcafonso.builtwithdark.com/react-query-paginated?page=0&results=10` endpoint will return a `200 OK` response with the `pageOneData` object, while a `GET` request for the `https://danieljcafonso.builtwithdark.com/react-query-paginated?page=1&results=10` endpoint will return a `200 OK` response with the `pageTwoData` object.

Now that we are sure that our components will always receive the same data after a request, we can write our tests and look at the `PaginatedQuery` component from a user-centric perspective; here are the test scenarios that you might identify:

- **As a user, I want to see that my data has loaded after opening the page**: In this scenario, we want our component to be rendered and check whether the initial loading data message shows up.

- **As a user, I want to see an error message if my data fails to load**: In this scenario, we want our component to render and see whether it shows the error message when the request fails.

- **As a user, I want to see the initially fetched data**: In this scenario, we want our component to render and wait until the data of the first page is fetched.

- **As a user, I want to click on the Next Page button and see the data from the next page**: In this scenario, we want our component to be rendered, ensure we have the initial data, and after clicking on the **Next Page** button, wait until the data of the second page is fetched.

- **As a user, I want to see a fetching indicator while fetching new data**: In this scenario, we want our component to be rendered, ensure we have the initial data, and after clicking on the **Next Page** button, ensure that the fetching indicator is rendered.

- **As a user, I want my data to show up while clicking on Next Page and Previous Page**: In this scenario, we want our component to be rendered, ensure we have the initial data, and after clicking on the **Next Page** button, ensure the second page shows up. We then click on the **Previous Page** button and ensure that the data of the first page is rendered again.

- **As a user, I want my Previous Page button to be disabled when I'm on the first page**: In this scenario, we want our component to be rendered and ensure we have the initial data. Since we are on the first page, we want our **Previous Page** button to be disabled.

- **As a user, I want my Next Page button to be disabled while waiting for new data to show up**: In this scenario, we want our component to render and ensure we have the initial data. After clicking the **Next Page** button, we need to ensure that this button is disabled.

With these scenarios in mind, this is the code we would write to test the `PaginatedQuery` component:

```
import PaginatedQuery from "../PaginatedQuery";
import { render, screen } from "../utils/test-utils";
import userEvent from "@testing-library/user-event";
import { server } from "../mocks/server";
import { rest } from "msw";

describe("PaginatedQuery tests", () => {
  test("should render loading indicator on start", () => {
    render(<PaginatedQuery />);
    expect(screen.getByText("Loading initial data...")).
      toBeInTheDocument();
  });

  test("should render error on failed fetching", async () => {
    server.use(rest.get("*", (req, res, ctx) =>
      res(ctx.status(403))));
    render(<PaginatedQuery />);

    expect(
      await screen.findByText("Request failed with status
        code 403")
    ).toBeInTheDocument();
  });

  test("should render first page data", async () => {
    render(<PaginatedQuery />);

    const firstName = await screen.findByText(/first1/i);
    expect(firstName).toBeInTheDocument();
    expect(screen.getByText(/last1/i)).toBeInTheDocument();
  });

  test("should render second page data", async () => {
    render(<PaginatedQuery />);
```

```js
    const firstName = await screen.findByText(/first1/i);
    expect(firstName).toBeInTheDocument();

    const nextPageButton = screen.getByRole("button", {
      name: "Next Page" });
    userEvent.click(nextPageButton);

    const secondPageFirstName = await screen.findByText
      (/first2/i);
    expect(secondPageFirstName).toBeInTheDocument();
    expect(screen.getByText(/last2/i)).toBeInTheDocument();
});

test("should show fetching indicator while fetching
  data", async () => {
    render(<PaginatedQuery />);

    const firstName = await screen.findByText(/first1/i);
    expect(firstName).toBeInTheDocument();

    const nextPageButton = screen.getByRole("button", {
      name: "Next Page" });
    userEvent.click(nextPageButton);

    expect(screen.getByText("Loading...")).
      toBeInTheDocument();
});

test("should change pages back and forth and render
  expected data", async () => {
    render(<PaginatedQuery />);

    expect(await screen.findByText(/first1/i)).
      toBeInTheDocument();
    expect(screen.getByText(/last1/i)).toBeInTheDocument();
```

```
    const nextPageButton = screen.getByRole("button", {
      name: "Next Page" });
    userEvent.click(nextPageButton);

    expect(await screen.findByText(/first2/i)).
      toBeInTheDocument();
    expect(screen.getByText(/last2/i)).toBeInTheDocument();

    const previousPageButton = screen.getByRole("button", {
      name: "Previous Page",
    });
    userEvent.click(previousPageButton);

    expect(await screen.findByText(/first1/i)).
      toBeInTheDocument();
    expect(screen.getByText(/last1/i)).toBeInTheDocument();
  });

  test("should have previous page button disabled on first
    page", async () => {
    render(<PaginatedQuery />);

    const previousPageButton = await screen.findByRole
      ("button", {
      name: "Previous Page",
    });

    expect(previousPageButton).toBeDisabled();
  });

  test("should have next page button disabled while
    changing pages", async () => {
    render(<PaginatedQuery />);

    const nextPageButton = await screen.findByRole
      ("button", {
```

```
    name: "Next Page",
  });
  userEvent.click(nextPageButton);

  expect(nextPageButton).toBeDisabled();
  });
});
```

1. We start by doing the necessary imports:

    I. Our `PaginatedQuery` component.

    II. Our `render` and `screen` utils from `test-utils`.

    III. The `userEvent` util from the `user-event` companion from the testing library. One thing to be aware of here is that we are using a user-event version before v14.

    IV. Our MSW `server` so that we can create a custom response mock for one of our test scenarios.

    V. The MSW `rest` namespace to create relevant request handlers for one of our test scenarios.

2. We create our test suite and, inside it, our tests:

    I. For the `"should render loading indicator on start"` test, we do the following:

    i. Render our `PaginatedQuery` component.

    ii. Leverage the `getByText` query to assert that the `"Loading initial data..."` message is on the DOM.

    II. For the `"should render error on failed fetching"` test, we do the following:

    i. Leverage our `server use` function to add a request handler to our current server instance. In this scenario, we add a handler that will catch every GET request (`"*"` indicates that this handler will match every route) and return `403 Forbidden` so that our request fails. Don't worry about this leaking into other tests because we made sure to call the `resetHandlers` function in our `setupTests` file. This will ensure that this custom request handler will only be used on this test.

    ii. Render our `PaginatedQuery` component.

    iii. Leverage the `findByText` query to `await` until the error message shows up on the DOM.

III. For the "should render first page data" test, we do the following:

  i. Render our `PaginatedQuery` component.
  ii. Wait until the data from the first name property from the first page shows up on the DOM.
  iii. Assert that the last name property also shows up on the DOM.

IV. For the "should render second page data" test, we do the following:

  i. Render our `PaginatedQuery` component.
  ii. Wait until the data from the first page shows up on the DOM.
  iii. Leverage the `getByRole` query to get a button with the text **Next Page** in it.
  iv. Click on the **Next Page** button.
  v. Wait until the data from the first name property from the second page shows up on the DOM.
  vi. Assert that the last name property from the second page also shows up on the DOM.

V. For the "should show fetching indicator while fetching data" test, we do the following:

  i. Render our `PaginatedQuery` component.
  ii. Wait until the data from the first page shows up on the DOM.
  iii. Leverage the `getByRole` query to get a button with the text **Next Page** in it and click on it.
  iv. Assert that our query is being fetched by using a `getByText` query to check whether the `"Loading..."` indicator shows up on the DOM.

VI. For the "should change pages back and forth and render expected data" test, we do the following:

  i. Render our `PaginatedQuery` component.
  ii. Wait until the data from the first page shows up on the DOM and assert that it is there.
  iii. Leverage the `getByRole` query to get a button with the text **Next Page** in it and click on it.
  iv. Wait until the data from the second page shows up on the DOM and assert that it is there.
  v. Leverage the `getByRole` query to get a button with the text **Previous Page** in it and click on it.
  vi. Wait until the data from the first page shows up on the DOM and assert that it is there.

VII. For the `"should have previous page button disabled on first page"` test, we do the following:

  i. Render our `PaginatedQuery` component.

  ii. Leverage the `findByRole` query to wait until the **Previous Page** button appears on the DOM.

  iii. Assert that the button is disabled.

VIII. For the `"should have next page button disabled while changing pages"` test, we do the following:

  i. Render our `PaginatedQuery` component.

  ii. Leverage the `findByRole` query to wait until the **Next Page** button shows up on the DOM and click on it.

  iii. Assert that the **Next Page** button is now disabled.

As you can see, we can test our queries in a fully user-centric approach and forget the implementation details. Now, let's move into the mutation section and see how it gets a bit harder to follow a user-centric approach.

Testing mutations

You can definitely follow a user-centric approach with mutations, although, in some scenarios, this might be harder. Let us review a component we wrote in *Chapter 6* and see how it might be harder for us to test it following a user-centric approach:

```
export const SimpleMutation = () => {
  const [name, setName] = useState("");

  const { mutate, isPaused } = useMutation({
    mutationFn: createUser,
  });

  const submitForm = (e) => {
    e.preventDefault();
    mutate({ name, age: 0 });
  };

  return (
    <div>
```

```
      {isPaused && <p> Waiting for network to come back </p>}
      <form>
        <input
          name="name"
          type={"text"}
          onChange={(e) => setName(e.target.value)}
          value={name}
        />
        <button disabled={isPaused} onClick={submitForm}>
          Add
        </button>
      </form>
    </div>
  );
};
```

In the preceding snippet, we can see our `SimpleMutation` component. Now, let us try to do our user-centric approach exercise and understand which test scenarios we could write:

- **As a user, I want to see a paused indicator when my mutation enters the paused state**: In this scenario, we want to render our component and, when we attempt to perform our mutation, the paused indicator message to appear.
- **As a user, I want to create data on the server**: In this scenario, we want to render our component, fill out the form, and then perform our mutation. But wait – how does our user assert this?

As you can see, the last scenario had an issue – a lack of information from the UI that our mutation was performed successfully.

Usually, an issue of this sort would be fixed by adding a notification for a user, informing them that the mutation was performed successfully. Letting the user know the mutation succeeded is always a good practice. Following this approach, our test would resemble something like this:

- **As a user, I want to create data on the server successfully**: In this scenario, we want to render our component, fill out the form, press the **Add** button, and wait for a success message to appear

As you can see, now we have a user-centric way to test our mutation. However, for some reason, let us assume that we cannot perform changes to our `SimpleMutation` component. How would we ensure that our mutation was performed? We would have to resort to implementation details. Our test scenario would resemble something like this:

- **As a user, I want to perform a mutation**: In this scenario, we want to render our component, fill out the form, press the **Add** button, and assert that our mutation was triggered

In this section, we will show you how to write tests for instances where the ideal (user-centric) approach is not something we can employ.

The first thing we need to do before we write our test is to make sure MSW intercepts our request and is successful:

```
rest.post("*/name-api/*", (req, res, ctx) => {
    return res(
      ctx.status(201),
      ctx.json({
        hello: "user",
      })
    );
})
```

In the preceding snippet, we create a request handler to add to our `handlers` array, which does the following.

Whenever we intercept a `POST` request to an endpoint that includes the `/name-api/` path, we return a `201 Created` response that will have an object in its body, with a `hello` property containing a string.

We can now write our tests for our `SimpleMutation` component. Just to recap, here are the tests we will be performing:

- As a user, I want to see a paused indicator when my mutation enters the paused state
- As a user, I want to perform a mutation

Let us now see our created test file:

```
import { axiosInstance } from "../api/userAPI";
import { SimpleMutation } from "../Mutation";
import { render, screen, waitFor } from
  "../utils/test-utils";
```

```js
import userEvent from "@testing-library/user-event";

const postSpy = jest.spyOn(axiosInstance, "post");

describe("SimpleMutation Tests", () => {
  test("data should be sent to the server", async () => {
    const name = "Daniel";
    render(<SimpleMutation />);
    const input = screen.getByRole("textbox");
    userEvent.type(input, name);
    userEvent.click(
      screen.getByRole("button", {
        name: /add/i,
      })
    );
    await waitFor(() =>
      expect(postSpy.mock.calls[0][1]).toEqual
        ({ name, age: 0 })
    );
  });

  test("on no network should display paused information", async () => {
    jest.spyOn(navigator, "onLine", "get").mockReturnValue
      (false);
    render(<SimpleMutation />);
    userEvent.click(
      screen.getByRole("button", {
        name: /add/i,
      })
    );
    const text = await screen.findByText("Waiting for
      network to come back");
    expect(text).toBeInTheDocument();
  });
});
```

Let us now review what we are doing in the preceding snippet:

1. We import our `axiosInstance` from our API file, as well as the `SimpleMutation` component we saw in *Chapter 6*, our custom `render` function, the `screen` object, and the `waitFor` function from our `test-utils`. Finally, we import the `userEvent` util from the `user-event` companion in the testing library.

   One thing to be aware of here is that we are using a user-event version before v14.

2. Since we will tie one of our tests to implementation details, we create `jest spy` over the `post` function of our `axiosInstance`. This means we can check whether our `post` function was called without replacing its implementation.

3. We create our test suite, and inside it, our tests:

   I. For the `"data should be sent to the server"` test, we do the following:

      i. Create a variable to hold the name we will use in our mutation.

      ii. Render our `SimpleMutation` component.

      iii. Leverage a `getByRole` query to get our name input.

      iv. Leverage the `type` event from `userEvent` and type our name inside our input.

      v. Leverage the `click` event from `userEvent` and click on the **Add text** button.

      vi. We then wait until the `post` function of our `axiosInstance` is called with the data from our mutation.

   II. For the `"on no network should display paused information"` test, we do the following:

      i. Since we want to make sure that we simulate being offline, we leverage the `mockReturnValue` function from the `spyOn` function to make sure we force our `navigator onLine` property to return `false`. This will make sure that our code is aware of being offline.

      ii. Render our `SimpleMutation` component.

      iii. Leverage the `click` event from the `userEvent` and click on the **Add text** button.

      iv. Since React Query will now know it's offline, the `isPaused` property is `true`. Therefore, we wait until the `"Waiting for network to come back"` message appears. We then assert it is on the DOM.

From the previous test, we learned that we can leverage `Jest` spies to check whether our function was called and make sure our mutation is performed. This doesn't guarantee how our component will behave when our mutation is successful because we don't have anything rendered in there to let us know. In the first case scenario, always ensure you have all the information your user needs so they can know that your mutation was successful. If you do this, you can test it in a user-centric way and avoid implementation details.

One mutation case that might be relevant for testing is when we perform an optimistic update. However, since we applied one of the aforementioned patterns in this chapter to it, we will be able to test it with the **React Hooks Testing Library** in the next section.

Testing custom hooks that use React Query

During development, there will be times when your custom hooks are too complex to test alongside the component that leverages them. This can be due to the size of the hook, complex logic, or just too many scenarios that would increase your test complexity if you focused on a user-centric approach. To fix this issue, the React Hooks Testing Library was created.

Now, it might be very tempting to go ahead and use this everywhere, but don't forget that a user-centric approach will ultimately help you to find issues faster and save time if you decide to refactor the way your hooks work. Either way, if your hook is not used alongside a component or is too complex, the React Hooks Testing Library is definitely something to consider.

Here is how to add the React Hooks Testing Library to your project:

- If you are running npm in your project, run the following command:

    ```
    npm install @testing-library/react-hooks react-test-renderer --save-dev
    ```

- If you are using Yarn, run the following command:

    ```
    yarn add @testing-library/react-hooks react-test-renderer --dev
    ```

- If you are using pnpm, run the following command:

    ```
    pnpm add @testing-library/react-hooks react-test-renderer --save-dev
    ```

If you are using React from version 18 and above, there is something to be aware of here. You don't need to install the React Hooks Testing Library, as from version 13.1.0 onward, the React Testing Library includes `renderHook`, which works similarly to the one from the React Hooks Testing Library.

As mentioned at the end of the last section, we will see how to test optimistic updates. Before we write our tests, let us see how our code looks after applying the patterns mentioned in this chapter.

To do this, we will leverage the `useOptimisticUpdateUserCreation` hook shown previously:

```
import { useMutation, useQueryClient } from
  "@tanstack/react-query";
import { userKeys } from "../../utils/queryKeyFactories";
import { createUser } from "../../api/userAPI";

const useOptimisticUpdateUserCreation = () => {
  const queryClient = useQueryClient();

  return useMutation({
    mutationFn: createUser,
    retry: 0,
    onSettled: () => queryClient.invalidateQueries
      (userKeys.all()),
    onMutate: async (user) => {
      await queryClient.cancelQueries(userKeys.all());

      const previousUsers = queryClient.getQueryData
        (userKeys.all());

      queryClient.setQueryData(userKeys.all(), (prevData) => [
        user,
        ...prevData,
      ]);

      return { previousUsers };
    },
    onError: (error, user, context) => {
      queryClient.setQueryData(userKeys.all(),
        context.previousUsers);
    },
  });
};

export default useOptimisticUpdateUserCreation;
```

Considering we already have the route leveraged in this hook handled by MSW, we can start considering our tests.

These are the scenarios we will be considering:

- **I want to perform an optimistic update right after triggering my mutation**: In this scenario, we render our hook, trigger our mutation, and wait until the query data affected by our mutation is updated.
- **I want my optimistic update data to be reverted after my mutation fails**: In this scenario, we render our hook and trigger our mutation, and when our mutation fails, our query data must stay the same as before the mutation was triggered.
- **I want my query to be invalidated after my mutation settles**: In this scenario, we render our hook and trigger our mutation. Once our mutation settles, we check whether our query was invalidated.

With these scenarios in mind, we can create our tests. This is what our test file would look like:

```
import useOptimisticUpdateUserCreation from
  "../useOptimisticUpdateUserCreation";
import { QueryClient, QueryClientProvider } from
  "@tanstack/react-query";
import { renderHook } from "@testing-library/react-hooks";
import { userKeys } from "../../../utils/
  queryKeyFactories";
import { server } from "../../../mocks/server";
import { rest } from "msw";

const queryClient = new QueryClient({
  logger: {
    log: console.log,
    warn: console.warn,
    error: jest.fn(),
  },
});
const wrapper = ({ children }) => (
  <QueryClientProvider client={queryClient}>{children}
    </QueryClientProvider>
);
```

```
describe("useOptimisticUpdateUserCreation", () => {
  test("should perform optimistic update", async () => {
    queryClient.setQueryData(userKeys.all(), []);
    const name = "user";
    const age = 20;
    const { result, waitFor } = renderHook(
      () => useOptimisticUpdateUserCreation(),
      {
        wrapper,
      }
    );

    result.current.mutate({ name, age });

    await waitFor(() =>
      expect(queryClient.getQueryData(userKeys.all())).
        toEqual([{ name, age }])
    );
  });

  test("should revert optimistic update", async () => {
    queryClient.setQueryData(userKeys.all(), []);
    server.use(rest.post("*", (req, res, ctx) =>
      res(ctx.status(403))));
    const name = "user";
    const age = 20;

    const { result, waitFor } = renderHook(() =>
      useOptimisticUpdateUserCreation(), {
      wrapper,
    });

    result.current.mutate({ name, age });

    await waitFor(() => expect(result.current.isError).
      toBe(true));
```

```
      await waitFor(() =>
        expect(queryClient.getQueryData(userKeys.all())).
          toEqual([])
      );
    });

    test("should invalidate query on settled", async () => {
      queryClient.setQueryData(userKeys.all(), []);
      const invalidateQueriesSpy = jest.spyOn(queryClient,
        "invalidateQueries");
      const name = "user";
      const age = 20;

      const { result, waitFor } = renderHook(
        () => useOptimisticUpdateUserCreation(),
        {
          wrapper,
        }
      );

      result.current.mutate({ name, age });

      await waitFor(() => expect(result.current.isSuccess).
        toBe(true));
      expect(invalidateQueriesSpy).toHaveBeenCalledWith
        (userKeys.all());
    });
  });
```

Let us now review what we do in the preceding snippet:

1. We start by doing the necessary imports:

    I. Our useOptimisticUpdateUserCreation custom hook.

    II. Our QueryClient and QueryClientProvider. Remember that we won't use the previously created customRender, so we must create a new wrapper here.

    III. renderHook from the React Hooks Testing Library. If you use renderHook from the React Testing Library, import it there instead.

IV. Our `userKeys` factory.

V. Our MSW `server` so that we can create a custom response mock for one of our test scenarios.

VI. The MSW `rest` namespace to create relevant request handlers for one of our test scenarios.

2. We create our `QueryClient` instance and pass it to our `wrapper`. This will be used to wrap our hook to use React Query.

3. We create our test suite and, inside it, our tests:

    I. For the `"should perform optimistic update"` test, we do the following:

        i. Ensure our cached query data for the query key under the `userKeys.all()` key is an empty array.

        ii. Create the `name` and `age` variables to avoid magic numbers in our test.

        iii. Render our hook and destructure the `waitFor` function and the `result` object from it.

        iv. We leverage our `result` object to access our `mutate` function and perform our mutation.

        v. We use the `waitFor` function to loop our assertion until it evaluates to `true`. In this scenario, we wait until the query cache has the optimistically updated data cached under the `userKeys.all()` query key.

    II. For the `"should revert optimistic update"` test, we do the following:

        i. Ensure our cached query data for the query key under the `userKeys.all()` key is an empty array.

        ii. Leverage our `server use` function to add a request handler to our current server instance. In this scenario, we add a handler that will catch every POST request (`"*"` indicates that this handler will match every route) and return a `403 Forbidden` so that our request fails. Don't worry about this leaking into other tests because we made sure to call the `resetHandlers` function in our `setupTests` file. This will ensure that this custom request handler will only be used on this test.

        iii. Create the `name` and `age` variables to avoid magic numbers in our test.

        iv. Render our hook and destructure the `waitFor` function and the `result` object from it.

        v. Leverage our `result` object to access our `mutate` function and perform our mutation.

        vi. Use the `waitFor` function to wait until our hook's `isError` property is `true`.

        vii. Once we are sure our mutation has failed, we again leverage the `waitFor` function to wait until the query data cached under the `userKeys.all()` key is the empty array we had before our mutation.

III. For the `"should invalidate query on settled"` test, we do the following:

   i. Ensure our cached query data for the query key under the `userKeys.all()` key is an empty array.

   ii. Since we are not rendering a query to make sure it is updating after our mutation, we create `invalidateQueriesSpy` over our `queryClient invalidateQueries` method.

   iii. Create the `name` and `age` variables to avoid magic numbers in our test.

   iv. Render our hook and destructure the `waitFor` function and the `result` object from it.

   v. Leverage our `result` object to access our `mutate` function and perform our mutation.

   vi. Wait until our `isSuccess` is `true`. This means our mutation was successful.

   vii. If our mutation is successful, we can assert that `invalidateQueriesSpy` was called with the `userKeys.all()`. This means that our `onSettled` function was called, and our query would be invalidated afterward.

We have now handled how to test custom hooks with React Hooks Testing Library. It is all about rendering your hook and leveraging its result to access what your hook returns to perform your actions and assertions.

Just for the sake of convenience and so that you can see a scenario where we test a query, let us see how we would test the `useMultipleQueriesV2` hook we saw in the *Checking whether data is fetched* section.

For this hook, we would only need a single test scenario:

- **I want my parallel queries to fetch data**: In this scenario, we render our hook and wait until it returns the data for the three queries it fetches

Like the previous hook, we have already set up our MSW request handlers previously, so we don't need to worry about them.

Let us look at the test file for our `useMultipleQueriesV2` hook:

```
import useMultipleQueriesV2 from "../useMultipleQueriesV2";
import { QueryClient, QueryClientProvider } from
   "@tanstack/react-query";
import { renderHook } from "@testing-library/react-hooks";

const queryClient = new QueryClient();
const wrapper = ({ children }) => (
  <QueryClientProvider client={queryClient}>{children}
    </QueryClientProvider>
```

```
);

describe("useMultipleQueriesV2", () => {
  test("should fetch all data", async () => {
    const { result, waitFor } = renderHook(() =>
      useMultipleQueriesV2(), {
      wrapper,
    });
    await waitFor(() =>
      expect(result.current.multipleQueries[0].data.hello).
        toBeDefined()
    );

    expect(result.current.multipleQueries[0].data.hello).
      toBe("userOne");
    expect(result.current.multipleQueries[1].data.hello).
      toBe("userTwo");
    expect(result.current.multipleQueries[2].data.hello).
      toBe("userThree");
  });
});
```

Let us now review what we are doing in the preceding snippet:

1. We start by doing the necessary imports:

    I.   Our useMultipleQueriesV2 custom hook.

    II. Our QueryClient and QueryClientProvider.

    III. renderHook from the React Hooks Testing Library. If you are using renderHook from the React Testing Library, import it from there instead.

2. We create our QueryClient instance and pass it to our wrapper. This will be used to wrap our hook to use React Query.

3. We create our test suite and, inside it, our test:

    - For the "should fetch all data" test, we do the following:

        i. Render our hook with the renderHook function and destructure the result object and the waitFor function from it.

ii. Wait until the data for the first query is defined.

iii. Given that the data is now defined, we assert that the `hello` property from the returned object on the first query has `userOne`.

iv. We also assert that the `hello` property from the returned object on the second query has `userTwo`.

v. We also assert that the `hello` property from the returned object on the third query has `userThree`.

As you can see, testing hooks and leveraging queries is much simpler, as it mostly only involves rendering and asserting. This a test example, where I did not test the hook because testing the component using it is much easier. Just check the test we did for it in the *Checking whether data is fetched* section.

With all this knowledge in mind, you should be able to write your code and then sleep amazingly well at night because you also wrote valuable tests, ensuring that nothing will break.

Summary

In this chapter, we learned how to test our components and hooks that leverage React Query. Congratulations! Thanks to this chapter, you have become a full-on React Query master!

You learned how MSW can save you a lot of time developing and testing your React Query code by having a couple of request handlers.

You got to meet the three patterns you can apply to make your code more readable and reusable (creating an API file, leveraging query key factories, and creating a hooks folder) and saw how valuable they were in adapting the code we saw in previous chapters.

Finally, you learned when to use the React Testing Library and the React Hooks Testing Library to test your queries and mutations, and you will keep the user-centric approach at the forefront of your mind when writing tests from now on.

Once again, congratulations! You should now be able to leverage React Query in every scenario and sleep better at night because you can write valuable tests for it. Now, run with this knowledge, and go ahead and convince your teammates about the value of the amazing TanStack Query and how its React Adapter, called React Query, will make their server state management much easier.

9
What Changes in React Query v5?

At the time of writing, version 5.0.0-alpha.1 of @tanstack/react-query has just been released. While it might take a couple of weeks for the stable version to be released, when this book is published, it might already be the version that installs by default every time you add React Query to your project.

To make sure you understand the changes that the content of this book may undergo after v5 is released, this bonus chapter was added.

This chapter might also serve as a helper to guide you when migrating from v4 to v5.

Once again, as a disclaimer, *the snippets of this chapter were tested on version 5.0.0-alpha.1 of @tanstack/react-query. Some of these things might still change, or some new ones might show up*. Either way, the snippets will be kept updated online in the next couple of months until a stable version is released. You can find them on the GitHub repository mentioned in the *Technical requirements* section.

By the end of this chapter, you will be aware of all the changes in React Query v5 that will have an impact on some of the things in this book.

In this chapter, we'll be covering the following topics:

- What are the support changes?
- Using only the object format
- Removing the logger
- Renaming `loading` to `pending`
- Renaming `cacheTime` to `gcTime`
- Renaming `Hydrate` to `HydrationBoundary`
- Removing `keepPreviousData` and using `placeholderData`

- Introducing a new way to do optimistic updates
- Introducing `maxPages` to infinite queries

Technical requirements

All the code examples for this chapter can be found on GitHub at `https://github.com/PacktPublishing/State-management-with-React-Query/tree/feat/chapter_9`.

What are the support changes?

The first thing to be aware of here is that the browser support has changed. From v5, your browser needs to be compatible with the following configurations:

- The Google Chrome version needs to be at least version 84
- The Mozilla Firefox version needs to be at least version 90
- The Microsoft Edge version needs to be at least version 84
- The Safari version needs to be at least version 15
- The Opera version needs to be at least version 70

Now that we know the support changes, let's see what features changed from v4 to v5, starting with the object format for custom hooks and functions.

Using only the object format

In v4 of React Query, most custom hooks and functions were overloaded to support previous patterns. This means that in your code, both of the `useQuery` hooks in the following snippet would be the same thing:

```
const { data } = useQuery({
    queryKey: ["api"]
    queryFn: fetchData,
});
const { data } = useQuery(["api"], fetchData);
```

As you can see from the preceding snippet, we create a query with `queryKey` `["api"]` and `queryFn` `fetchData` twice. This is because the second and first examples are just instances of the same hook that has been overloaded.

With the introduction of v5, the second example shown in the preceding snippet is no longer supported; therefore, you can only use your hooks by passing them a single object with the needed options. Here is the syntax that you need to follow from now on:

```
useQuery({ queryKey, queryFn, ...options })
useMutation({ mutationFn, ...options })
useInfiniteQuery({ queryKey, queryFn, ...options })
```

As you can see from the preceding snippet, we have three React Query hooks, and each one of them receives a couple of things:

- The `useQuery` and `useInfiniteQuery` hooks need to receive `queryKey` and `queryFn` as required parameters. These hooks allow you to pass them some of the options you should already know from the previous chapters.
- The `useMutation` hook needs to receive `mutationFn` as a required parameter. It also allows you to pass it some of the options we learned about in *Chapter 6* when we saw what options our `useMutation` hook receives.

Luckily, throughout the book, we followed the object approach right from the beginning, so you should have followed the right approach from the start and won't suffer much from the change.

Another thing to be aware of is that this change applies to the `queryClient` functions. Functions such as `invalidateQueries`, `refetchQueries`, and `prefetchQuery` must also receive the expected object.

Now that you know about the single object format, we can look at one thing that was removed in v5 – `logger`.

Removing the logger

Previously, React Query logged failed queries to the console in the production environment. This quickly became an issue because our application users could see implementation detail errors that they shouldn't be aware of. To deal with this issue, the ability to create a custom logger was added, where you could override what React Query used for logging.

Recently, React Query removed all logging in production and improved their development logs. Given this scenario, in v5, `logger` was no longer needed and was removed.

From now on, `console` will be used as the default logger.

Now that you know this change, let's see the first renaming of v5 – `loading` to `pending`.

Renaming loading to pending

The `loading` status has caused some confusion. This is because most people associate it with data loading; secondly, if your query is disabled due to having the `enabled` option as `false`, it will show up as `loading`. To avoid more confusion and have a clearer name, the `loading` status has been renamed.

Here are the changes that have been applied:

- The `loading` status has been renamed `pending`
- The derived `isLoading` status has been renamed `isPending`
- A new derived `isLoading` flag has been added, which basically translates as the `isPending && isFetching` expression
- Considering that there was already a flag doing the same thing called `isInitialLoading`, the `isInitialLoading` flag has been deprecated

Let us now review `ComponentA`, which we saw in *Chapter 4*, and apply these changes:

```
const ComponentA = () => {
  const { data, error, isPending, isError, isFetching } =
    useQuery({
      queryKey: [{ queryIdentifier: "api", apiName: apiA }],
      queryFn: fetchData,
    });

  if (isPending) return <div> Loading data... </div>;
  ...
};
```

As you can see from the preceding snippet, all we have to do is rename `isLoading` `isPending`.

As for the behavior, it is also the same. What we have to be aware of here is that after the first query mounts when we don't have data, our `status` query will be `pending` instead of `loading`, as it was previously.

With this in mind, we can move to the next renaming of v5 – `cacheTime` is now `gcTime`.

Renaming cacheTime to gcTime

This was one of the changes I'm most personally happy about because it is probably the most misunderstood option in React Query. Most often, it is assumed that `cacheTime` means the length of time that data will be cached instead of what it really means, which is the time that inactive data in the cache will remain in memory.

To stop this misconception, the `cacheTime` option has been renamed `gcTime`. This is because gc is often a shortened way to refer to the garbage collector. Therefore, from now on, we explicitly declare the time until our data is garbage-collected.

To use it, all you need to do is add the `gcTime` option to your `useQuery/useMutation` hook, like this:

```
useQuery({
    gcTime: 60000
});
```

In the snippet, we define that after our query is inactive for one minute, the data will be garbage-collected.

To wrap up the renaming spree, let us see how our `Hydrate` component changed.

Renaming Hydrate to HydrationBoundary

When using the hydrate pattern in SSR, the `Hydrate` component was not fully descriptive about what it meant. To make it more concise and match other boundaries defined in TanStack Query, it was renamed `HydrationBoundary`. Due to this, you now have to rename it in your Next.js or Remix code.

Let us now see how the snippets change.

Next.js hydrate pattern renaming

This is what our Next.js _app component will look like now:

```
import { useState } from "react";
import {
  HydrationBoundary,
  QueryClient,
  QueryClientProvider,
} from "@tanstack/react-query";
```

```
export default function App({ Component, pageProps }) {
  const [queryClient] = useState(() => new QueryClient());

  return (
  <QueryClientProvider client={queryClient}>
    <HydrationBoundary state={pageProps.
        dehydratedState}>
      <Component {...pageProps} />
    </HydrationBoundary>
  </QueryClientProvider>
  );
}
```

As you can see from the preceding snippet, all we have to do is rename `Hydrate` to `HydrationBoundary`. Everything else remains the same.

Remix hydrate pattern changes

This is what our Remix root component will look like now:

```
import {
  ...
  Outlet,
} from "@remix-run/react";
import { useState } from "react";
import {
  HydrationBoundary,
  QueryClient,
  QueryClientProvider,
} from "@tanstack/react-query";
import { useDehydratedState } from "use-dehydrated-state";

export default function App() {
  const [queryClient] = useState(() => new QueryClient());
  const dehydratedState = useDehydratedState();

  return (
  ...
```

```
      <QueryClientProvider client={queryClient}>
        <HydrationBoundary state={dehydratedState}>
          <Outlet />
        </HydrationBoundary>
      </QueryClientProvider>
    ...
  );
}
```

As you can see from the preceding snippet, and just as we saw in the Next.js example, all we have to do is rename `Hydrate` to `HydrationBoundary`. Everything else remains the same.

Now that you know this change, let us look at something that impacted how we do paginated queries.

Removing keepPreviousData and using placeholderData

The `keepPreviousData` option and the `isPreviousData` flags have been removed. This is because they did almost the same task as the `placeholderData` option and the `isPlaceholderData` flag.

So that `placeholderData` can fully do exactly the same thing as `keepPreviousData`, the previous query data was added as an argument to the `placeholderData` function. This now means that by leveraging the `keepPreviousData` custom function from React Query, `useQuery` will allow `placeholderData` to work the same way as `keepPreviousData` did previously.

Let us see how our `PaginatedQuery` code changes in v5:

```
import { useQuery, keepPreviousData } from "@tanstack/react-query";
...
const PaginatedQuery = () => {
  ...
  const { isPending, isError, error, data, isFetching,
    isPlaceholderData } =
    useQuery({
      queryKey: userKeys.paginated(page),
      queryFn: fetchData,
      placeholderData: keepPreviousData,
    });

  if (isPending) {
```

```
        return <h2>Loading initial data...</h2>;
    }

    ...

    return (
        <>
            ...
            <button
                disabled={isPlaceholderData}
                onClick={() => setPage((old) => old + 1)}
            >
                Next Page
            </button>
            ...
        </>
    );
};

export default PaginatedQuery;
```

In the preceding snippet, we changed our `PaginatedQuery` component to adapt to the changes necessary due to the removal of the `keepPreviousData` option. This is what we do:

1. We import our `keepPreviousData` helper from React Query.
2. Since we need to refactor the component, we rename `isLoading` to `isPending`.
3. We rename `isPreviousData` to `isPlaceholderData`.
4. We rename the `keepPreviousData` option to `placeholderData` and pass it the `keepPreviousData` helper.

Now, v5 did not only remove and rename things. It also added some new things, including a new way to perform optimistic updates.

Introducing a new way to perform optimistic updates

When performing optimistic updates, you must always be careful about the changes you make to your cache. One typo or mistake might accidentally impact other queries outside of the one you want to change initially.

Fortunately, with v5, TanStack Query has introduced a way to perform optimistic updates where you can fully rely on your UI and stop changing your cache.

Let us see how:

```
export const NewOptimisticMutation = () => {
  const [name, setName] = useState("");
  const [age, setAge] = useState(0);
  const queryClient = useQueryClient();

  const { data } = useQuery({
    queryKey: userKeys.all(),
    queryFn: fetchAllData,
    retry: 0,
  });

  const mutation = useMutation({
    mutationFn: createUser,
    onSettled: () =>
      queryClient.invalidateQueries({ queryKey: userKeys.
        all() }),
  });

  return (
    <div>
      {data?.map((user, index) => (
        <div key={user.userID + index}>
          Name: {user.name} Age: {user.age}
        </div>
      ))}
      {mutation.isPending && (
        <div key={String(mutation.submittedAt)}>
          Name: {mutation.variables.name} Age:
            {mutation.variables.age}
        </div>
      )}
      <form>
```

```
          <input
            name="name"
            type={"text"}
            onChange={(e) => setName(e.target.value)}
            value={name}
          />
          <input
            name="number"
            type={"number"}
            onChange={(e) => setAge(Number(e.target.value))}
            value={age}
          />
          <button
            disabled={mutation.isPaused ||
              mutation.isPending}
            type="button"
            onClick={(e) => {
              e.preventDefault();
              mutation.mutate({ name, age });
            }}
          >
            Add
          </button>
        </form>
      </div>
    );
};
```

In the preceding snippet, we can see the new way React Query allows us to perform optimistic updates. This is what we do:

1. Create state variables and respective setters for the name and age inputs.
2. Get access to our `queryClient`.
3. Create our query, using the query factory `all` function to give us the query key and `fetchAllData` as the `query` function.
4. Create our mutation, using `createUser` as the mutation function. Inside this mutation, we leverage the `onSettled` callback to invalidate our query.

5. In our component return, we create `div` with the following:

    I. We use `data` from our query to display our users' data.

    II. We use our mutation `isPending` flag to let us know whether we have any mutation currently being performed. If this flag is `true`, we can access and render our `mutation` variables on the DOM.

    III. We create our controlled form with our name and age inputs.

    IV. We also create a button that, upon `onClick`, will trigger our mutation with our name and age values.

As you can see now, we can perform mutations without changing our query cache data. This is super powerful and can save you a lot of unintentional headaches caused by messing up your cache.

By checking the code of the preceding snippet, one thing you might wonder is whether the mutation lives on the same component as the query. Does this mean that if you have a mutation that lives outside of the same place of your query, you won't be able to perform optimistic updates this way? It does not.

If you have a mutation performing somewhere else and want to perform an optimistic update, you can leverage the `useMutationState` custom hook.

Here is how:

```
export const NewOptimisticMutationV2 = () => {
  const { data } = useQuery({
    queryKey: userKeys.all(),
    queryFn: fetchAllData,
    retry: 0,
  });

  const [mutation] = useMutationState({
    filters: { mutationKey: userKeys.userMutation(),
      status: "pending" },
    select: (mutation) => ({
      ...mutation.state.variables,
      submittedAt: mutation.state.submittedAt,
    }),
  });

  return (
    <div>
```

```
      {data?.map((user, index) => (
        <div key={user.userID + index}>
          Name: {user.name} Age: {user.age}
        </div>
      ))}
      {mutation && (
        <div key={String(mutation.submittedAt)}>
          Name: {mutation.name} Age: {mutation.age}
        </div>
      )}
      <MutationForm />
    </div>
  );
};
```

In the preceding snippet, we have the `NewOptimisticMutationV2` component. In this component, we perform an optimistic update outside the component where your mutation lives. In this component, we render our query data and have the component where our mutation happens, called `MutationForm`, rendered as a child component.

Here is what we do in the `NewOptimisticMutationV2` component:

1. Create our query, using our query factory `all` function to give us the query key and `fetchAllData` as the query function.
2. Get access to our mutation by using the `useMutationState` hook.
3. With this hook, we access a mutation currently with the pending status and the `mutationKey` `userKeys.userMutation()` that comes from our query factory.
4. Then, leverage the `select` option from the `useMutationState` hook to get the `mutation` variables and the `submittedAt` property.
5. In our component return, we create a `div` with the following:
   I. We use `data` from our query to display our users' data.
   II. If we have any mutation currently being performed, we can access and render our `mutation` variables on the DOM.

I mentioned in the previous description that the mutation needs to have `mutationKey` to be able to be found. This is how to add it to your mutation:

```
const mutation = useMutation({
    mutationFn: createUser,
```

```
    mutationKey: userKeys.userMutation(),
});
```

As you can see from the preceding snippet, we added the `userKeys.userMutation()` key from our query factory and added it to our `useMutation` hook's `mutationKey` property.

Now that you know about the new way to perform optimistic updates, let us see what changed in our infinite queries.

Introducing maxPages to infinite queries

Infinite queries is an amazing pattern that helps you build infinite lists. However, there is one issue with it before v5 – all the fetched pages are cached in memory; therefore, the more pages you see, the more memory you consume.

To prevent this from happening and improve your user experience, the `maxPages` option was added to the `useInfiniteQuery` hook. This option limits the number of pages that will be stored in the query cache.

This is what our infinite query example, seen in *Chapter 5*, would look like now:

```
const {
    isPending,
    isError,
    error,
    data,
    fetchNextPage,
    isFetchingNextPage,
    hasNextPage,
} = useInfiniteQuery({
    queryKey: userKeys.api(),
    queryFn: getInfiniteData,
    defaultPageParam: 0,
    maxPages: 5,
    getNextPageParam: (lastPage, pages) => {
        return lastPage?.info?.nextPage;
    },
    getPreviousPageParam: (firstPage, pages) => {
        return firstPage?.info?.prevPage
    }
```

```
});

if (isPending) {
  return <h2>Loading initial data...</h2>;
}
...
```

In the preceding snippet, we can see our infinite query code refactor after v5 and leverage the `maxPages` option. Here is what changed:

1. We use `isPending` instead of `isLoading`
2. The `defaultPageParam` option indicates which is the default page that React Query will use to fetch the first page. This option is now required, so it was added.
3. We add `5` as our `maxPages` option. This means that only five pages will be stored in memory. Since we use this option, the `getPreviousPageParam` option is now required so that React Query can fetch pages in both directions if needed.

With this, we have now wrapped up all the relevant changes in React Query v5 that might impact this book.

Summary

In this chapter, we learned about all the changes v5 might bring to React Query. By now, you should know about the support changes you will need to be aware of in your browser and understand why we've always followed the object format throughout the book.

You've seen why `logger` was removed and understand why renaming `loading` to `pending` makes more sense.

Speaking of renaming, you won't be confused again because `gcTime` is a more accurate word than `cacheTime`, and `HydrationBoundary` represents better what it does than `Hydrate`.

You've learned that for paginated queries, the `placeholderData` option is the way to go and that `keepPreviousData` was removed.

Finally, you were introduced to a new way to perform optimistic updates without updating your cache and found a way to save memory in your infinite queries, by leveraging the `maxPages` option.

As you may recall from what I said previously, this was tested in an alpha version of React Query, so some of these things might still change.

It is exciting to see some of these changes, as they progressively improve the library.

Personally, I can't wait to see what comes next to TanStack Query. With every new version, it always finds a new way to make my life easier when dealing with server state. Hopefully, it will do the same for you from now on.

Index

A

AbortController 82
AbortSignal 82
API file
  creating 147, 148

C

cacheTime option 58, 115
cancelQueries method 84
client state 15, 19, 20
code, organizing 147
  API file, creating 147, 148
  hooks folder, creating 149-151
  query key factories, leveraging 148
Component A 19
Component B 19
components, with React Query
  mutations, testing 171-176
  testing 151
  testing, scenarios 153-171
  testing utils, setting up 151-153
content delivery network (CDN) 29
custom hooks, with React Query
  testing 176-184

D

data
  refetching, with useQuery hook 61
data variable 51, 52
data, with useQuery
  automatic refetching 61
  manual refetching 63
data with useQuery, automatic refetching
  options 62, 63
  query keys 61
data with useQuery, manual refetching
  QueryClient, using 63
  refetch function, using 63
dependent queries 64
  fetching, with useQuery 64, 65
Devtools
  used, for debugging queries 94-98
dynamic import 38

E

Embedded Mode 37, 38
enabled option 59
error variable 52

F

fetchStatus variable 55-57
Floating Mode 35, 36

G

global state 12-19
GraphQL 46

H

hooks folder
  creating 149-151
hydrate pattern
  applying, in Next.js 135-137
  applying, in Remix 137-141
  using 134

I

infinite queries 197
  creating 90-93
infinite scrolling 23
initialData pattern
  applying, in Next.js 131, 132
  applying, in Remix 132, 133
  using 131
inline function 48, 49
invalidateQueries 78-80

L

lazy loading 23

M

memo 19
MobX 12
Mock Service Worker
  configuring 144-146
MutationCache 30
mutation function 100
  example 100-103
mutation options 115
  cacheTime 115
  mutationKey 116
  onError 118
  onMutate 117
  onSettled 118, 119
  onSuccess 117, 118
  retry 116
  retryDelay 117
mutations 27
  testing 171-176

N

Next.js 129
  hydrate pattern, applying 135-137
  initialData pattern, applying 131, 132
Next.js hydrate pattern
  renaming 189, 190
npm
  React Query, installing 28

O

onError option 60, 118
onMutate option 117
onSettled option 118, 119

onSuccess option 60, 117, 118
optimistic updates 22
  performing 123-127

P

paginated data 23
paginated queries
  creating 86-89
parallel queries
  building 74
  building, dynamically 75, 76
  building, manually 74, 75
pnpm
  React Query, installing 29
prefetchQuery 80
production build
  React Query Devtools, enabling 38-40

Q

queries 26, 44
  debugging, with Devtools 94-98
QueryCache 30
Query cancelation 82-84
  automatic cancelation 84
  manual cancelation 84
QueryClient 30
  data, prefetching 80-82
  defaultOptions 33
  leveraging 76-78
  logger 32, 33
  MutationCache 31, 32
  QueryCache 31, 32
  QueryClientProvider 34
  Query invalidation 78, 79
  using 63

QueryFilters 77
query function 46-48
  inline function 48, 49
  QueryFunctionContext 49, 50
query key factories
  leveraging 148
query keys 44-46, 61

R

random property 45
React application
  state, managing 4-6
React Context
  state, sharing with 10-12
React Hooks 5
React Hooks Testing Library 176
React Query 5, 25, 26
  configuring 29
  features 27, 28
  installing 28
  installing, in npm 28
  installing, in pnpm 29
  installing, in script tag 29
  installing, in Yarn 29
  mutation 27
  query 26
  QueryClient 30
  QueryClientProvider 34
  solving, server state challenges 27, 28
  using, with SSR 130
React Query Devtools
  adding 34
  Embedded Mode 37, 38
  enabling, in production build 38-40
  Floating Mode 35, 36

React Query, using with GraphQL
   example 47
React Query, using with REST
   example 48
React Query v5, changes
   cacheTime option, renaming to gcTime option 189
   Hydrate component, renaming to HydrationBoundary component 189
   isPlaceholderData flag, using 191, 192
   keepPreviousData option, removing 191, 192
   loading status, renaming to pending status 188
   logger, removing 187
   maxPages, introducing to infinite queries 197, 198
   new way, to perform optimistic updates 192-197
   object format, using 186, 187
   support changes 186
reducer 8
Redux 12
Redux Saga 20
Redux Thunk 20
refetch function
   using 63
refetching 61
Remix 129
   hydrate pattern, applying 137-141
   initialData pattern, applying 132, 133
Remix hydrate pattern
   changes 190, 191
REST 46
retryDelay option 59, 117
retry option 58, 116

returns, useMutation
   data 108, 109
   error 109
   isPaused 114, 115
   mutate 103-105
   mutateAsync 106-108
   reset 110
   status 111-114

S

script tag
   React Query, installing 29
secondaryTheme 18, 19
server-side rendering (SSR) 129, 130
   React Query, using with 130
   using, advantages 130
server state 13, 15, 20, 21
server state, challenges 22
   caching 22
   optimistic updates 22
   performance optimization 23, 24
   requests, depuding 23
side-effect patterns
   additional side effect, performing 119, 120
   performing, after mutations 119
   query data update, performing after mutation 122
   query refetch, retriggering after mutation 121
staleTime option 58
state 3, 4
   in React application 4-6
   managing, with useReducer 8, 9
   managing, with useState 6-8
   sharing, with React Context 10-12

state management libraries
   similarities 12, 13
status variable 53-55
Suspense 39

T

TanStack Query 26
testing utils
   setting up 151-153

U

useEffect 18
useInfiniteQuery 90
useMemo 19
useMutation 100
   returns 103
   working 100
useQueries 44, 75
   implementing 65-71
   query function 44-48
   query key 44-46
   used, for fetching dependent queries 64, 65
useQuery hook
   used, for refetching data 61

useQuery hook, options
   cacheTime option 58
   enabled option 59
   onError option 60
   onSuccess option 60
   retryDelay option 59
   retry option 58
   staleTime option 58
useQuery hook, returns
   data variable 51, 52
   error variable 52
   fetchStatus variable 55-57
   status variable 53-55
useReducer
   using, to manage state 8, 9
useState
   using, to manage state 6-8

Y

Yarn
   React Query, installing 29

Z

Zustand 12

‹packt›

www.packtpub.com

Subscribe to our online digital library for full access to over 7,000 books and videos, as well as industry leading tools to help you plan your personal development and advance your career. For more information, please visit our website.

Why subscribe?

- Spend less time learning and more time coding with practical eBooks and Videos from over 4,000 industry professionals
- Improve your learning with Skill Plans built especially for you
- Get a free eBook or video every month
- Fully searchable for easy access to vital information
- Copy and paste, print, and bookmark content

Did you know that Packt offers eBook versions of every book published, with PDF and ePub files available? You can upgrade to the eBook version at www.packtpub.com and as a print book customer, you are entitled to a discount on the eBook copy. Get in touch with us at customercare@packtpub.com for more details.

At www.packtpub.com, you can also read a collection of free technical articles, sign up for a range of free newsletters, and receive exclusive discounts and offers on Packt books and eBooks.

Other Books You May Enjoy

If you enjoyed this book, you may be interested in these other books by Packt:

Full-Stack React Projects

Shama Hoque

ISBN: 9781839215414

- Extend a basic MERN-based application to build a variety of applications.
- Add real-time communication capabilities with Socket.IO.
- Implement data visualization features for React applications using Victory.
- Develop media streaming applications using MongoDB GridFS.
- Improve SEO for your MERN apps by implementing server-side rendering with data.
- Implement user authentication and authorization using JSON web tokens.
- Set up and use React 360 to develop user interfaces with VR capabilities.

React 17 Design Patterns and Best Practices

Carlos Santana Roldán

ISBN: 978-1-80056-044-4

- Get to grips with the techniques of styling and optimizing React components
- Create components using the new React Hooks
- Use server-side rendering to make applications load faster
- Get up to speed with the new React Suspense technique and using GraphQL in your projects
- Write a comprehensive set of tests to create robust and maintainable code.

Packt is searching for authors like you

If you're interested in becoming an author for Packt, please visit `authors.packtpub.com` and apply today. We have worked with thousands of developers and tech professionals, just like you, to help them share their insight with the global tech community. You can make a general application, apply for a specific hot topic that we are recruiting an author for, or submit your own idea.

Share your thoughts

Now you've finished *State Management with React Query*, we'd love to hear your thoughts! Scan the QR code below to go straight to the Amazon review page for this book and share your feedback or leave a review on the site that you purchased it from.

`https://packt.link/r/1-803-23134-3`

Your review is important to us and the tech community and will help us make sure we're delivering excellent quality content.

Download a free PDF copy of this book

Thanks for purchasing this book!

Do you like to read on the go but are unable to carry your print books everywhere?

Is your eBook purchase not compatible with the device of your choice?

Don't worry, now with every Packt book you get a DRM-free PDF version of that book at no cost.

Read anywhere, any place, on any device. Search, copy, and paste code from your favorite technical books directly into your application.

The perks don't stop there, you can get exclusive access to discounts, newsletters, and great free content in your inbox daily

Follow these simple steps to get the benefits:

1. Scan the QR code or visit the link below

```
https://packt.link/free-ebook/9781803231341
```

2. Submit your proof of purchase
3. That's it! We'll send your free PDF and other benefits to your email directly

Printed in Poland
by Amazon Fulfillment
Poland Sp. z o.o., Wrocław